Kathleen Conn

Bullying
and
Harassment

A Legal
Guide for
Educators

Association for Supervision and Curriculum Development
Alexandria, Virginia USA

Association for Supervision and Curriculum Development
1703 N. Beauregard St. • Alexandria, VA 22311-1714 USA
Phone: 800-933-2723 or 703-578-9600 • Fax: 703-575-5400
Web site: http://www.ascd.org • E-mail: member@ascd.org
Author guidelines: www.ascd.org/write

Gene R. Carter, *Executive Director;* Nancy Modrak, *Director of Publishing;* Julie Houtz, *Director of Book Editing & Production;* Tim Sniffin, *Project Manager;* Georgia McDonald, *Senior Graphic Designer;* Valerie Sprague, *Typesetter;* Eric Coyle, *Production Specialist*

Copyright © 2004 by the Association for Supervision and Curriculum Development (ASCD). All rights reserved. No part of this publication may be reproduced or transmitted in any form or by any means, electronic or mechanical, including photocopy, recording, or any information storage and retrieval system, without permission from ASCD. Readers who wish to duplicate material copyrighted by ASCD may do so for a small fee by contacting the Copyright Clearance Center (CCC), 222 Rosewood Dr., Danvers, MA 01923, USA (phone: 978-750-8400; fax: 978-646-8600; Web: http://www.copyright.com). ASCD has authorized the CCC to collect such fees on its behalf. Requests to reprint rather than photocopy should be directed to ASCD's permissions office at 703-578-9600.

Printed in the United States of America. Cover art copyright © 2004 by ASCD.

ASCD publications present a variety of viewpoints. The views expressed or implied in this book should not be interpreted as official positions of the Association.

All Web links in this book are correct as of the publication date below but may have become inactive or otherwise modified since that time. If you notice a deactivated or changed link, please e-mail books@ascd.org with the words "Link Update" in the subject line. In your message, please specify the Web link, the book title, and the page number on which the link appears.

ISBN-13: 978-1-4166-0014-5   ISBN-10: 1-4166-0014-0 • ASCD product 104147
s9/04
Also available as a PDF e-book through netLibrary, ebrary, and online booksellers that carry such e-books.

Library of Congress Cataloging-in-Publication Data
Conn, Kathleen, 1942-
  Bullying and harassment : a legal guide for educators / Kathleen Conn.
    p. cm.
  Includes bibliographical references.
  ISBN 1-4166-0014-0 (alk. paper)
  1. Sexual harassment in education--Law and legislation--United States. 2. Bullying in schools--United States. I. Title.

  KF4155.C66 2004
  344.73'079--dc22

                                                        2004013241

11 10 09 08 07 06 05   12 11 10 9 8 7 6 5 4 3 2

I dedicate this book to my husband,

Coulson A. Conn,

who seldom reads my completed articles or books,

but who patiently suffers throughout

their creation.

I also dedicate this book to the school bullies,

both students and adults, who gave me

the desire and determination to write this book.

May educators' knowledge of the law

assist their rehabilitation.

Bullying and Harassment

A Legal Guide for Educators

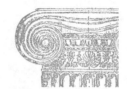

Foreword

IN THE YEARS SINCE THE APRIL 1999 SHOOTINGS AT COLUMBINE HIGH School in Littleton, Colorado, our nation has been obsessed with issuing school violence reports and taking measures that allegedly make schools safer than before. From passing state laws on bullying to suspending and expelling more and more students under the "one-strike, you are out" mentality of zero tolerance, the good senses of the legislative and educational establishments seem mislaid. One important thing that has gotten lost in this surge of reports and frenzy to reduce bullying in schools is the rights of students.

During an era when it is fashionable and all but permitted to ignore or abrogate the rights of students, Kathleen Conn has given us a book in which individual student rights are balanced with the rights of the group. Her book (re)turns our attention to gender-based and sexual harassment in elementary and secondary schools—problems all too real at both levels. Remarkable in its scope, Conn reviews, explains, and questions developments, legal and otherwise, in the fields of bullying, harassment, threats, and student rights.

Despite continuing guidance from the federal courts, including the U.S. Supreme Court, insights from surveys attesting to the issue's ugly entrenchment in our schools, and laws at both the federal and state levels that require attention and compliance from school officials, our nation's schools are riddled with examples of harassment. Conn takes the reader through a thicket of lawsuits with clarity and perspective. This book is well documented and researched, yet always offers simple and straightforward presentations of legal cases. Most remarkably, Conn provides multiple interpretations of legal decisions, giving the reader a chance to swirl around in the complexity of ideas that are often imbedded in any one judicial decision. Yet, all the while the legal explanations are written in an accessible, nonformidable manner.

Finally, Conn's book is up-to-date and very contemporary. She covers advances in the use of the Internet in schools and the tensions that may arise in a nation that values its freedoms of expression and speech. In addition, she points the reader towards abuses of zero tolerance and antibullying laws that have blanketed the nation's schools. She does not shy away from controversy.

I will be telling everyone I know who works in schools to read this book. Then together we can thank Kathleen Conn for giving us a great primer and review on rights in a democratic society.

—*Nan Stein*
Senior Researcher
Center for Research on Women
Wellesley College
Wellesley, Massachusetts
May 8, 2004

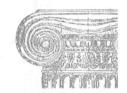

Acknowledgments

I WOULD LIKE TO THANK KENNETH LANE, DIRECTOR OF THE NATIONAL Center for Excellence in Learning, California State University, San Bernardino, California, for his encouragement and preliminary comments concerning my manuscript.

I also owe gratitude to Nan Stein for not only agreeing to write the Foreword of this book, but also for contributing valuable suggestions about remedies for bullying and sexual harassment.

I am grateful to my editor Tim Sniffin at ASCD for his light yet firm hand while helping to make this second book more reader friendly.

As always, I owe a special debt to my family for their support, their understanding, and their ongoing examples of kindness and sensitivity to the feelings of others.

I would especially like to thank my youngest son Kendric for sharing insightful and thought-provoking comments on discrimination and prejudice, several of which inspired paragraphs in the text.

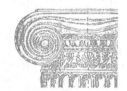

Introduction

FOR MANY ADULTS, THE MOST VIVID MEMORY FROM THEIR FORMER SCHOOL days involves a distinctly unpleasant incident or situation, with a bully often at the heart of the memory. Some adults may remember being the victim of a bully. Some may recall feeling forced to stand silently by while a good friend or a weaker colleague was the victim. Still others, a very small number of adults, may reflect with remorse that they were, indeed, the bullies who tormented and terrorized their schoolmates.

Bullying, however, has more far-reaching ramifications than simply contributing to unpleasant childhood memories. Many researchers have documented the association of bullying with other antisocial behaviors. The pioneering research of Dan Olweus in Norway and Sweden in the late 1980s and early 1990s documented that 60 percent of boys identified as bullies in grades 6–9 had at least one criminal conviction by age 24. Of these former middle school bullies, 35–40 percent were convicted of three or more serious crimes by their mid-twenties (Olweus, 1993). After Olweus' initial studies, bullying in schools soon began to receive attention in Japan, England, the Netherlands, Canada, Australia, and the United States. The National Center for Injury Prevention and Control (2004), a division of the Centers for Disease Control, cites bullying or being bullied as a "risk factor" for youth violence. An April 2003 report published by researchers from the National

Institute of Child Health and Human Development demonstrates a strong and consistent relationship between bullying and subsequent violent behaviors among U.S. children. Although this association was strongest for those who exhibited the bullying behaviors, both bullies and victims of bullying showed higher rates of weapon carrying, fighting, and being injured in fights in schools than those who were not bullies or victims. Clearly, bullying is a problem that schools must acknowledge and address.

Identifying a Bully

What is a "bully"? A typical bully is hard to describe; after all, bullies do not wear a capital *B* on their jackets. Psychologists and behavior specialists maintain that bullies come in all shapes and sizes. Students bully other students; students bully teachers. Teachers bully students; teachers bully other teachers and parents. Those with the power bully; those who feel *powerless* also bully.

Some generalizations, however, are noteworthy. Boys are more apt to bully than girls. Strong adolescent boys are more likely to bully weaker comrades. Boys and girls have different bullying "styles." Boys more often utilize physical force when bullying; girls, on the other hand, use relational tactics, shunning or excluding victims from "in-crowd" activities or opportunities. However, the school bully can even be the principal or a seemingly very popular teacher. Bullies do come in all guises.

Barbara Coloroso (2003), in her book *The Bully, the Bullied, and the Bystander*, defines bullying as "a conscious, willful, and deliberate hostile activity intended to harm, induce fear through the threat of further aggression, and create terror" (p. 13). Coloroso contends that four elements characterize all bullies, no matter what sex, age, or job title: (1) an imbalance of power, in which the bully is bigger, stronger, or more favorably situated than the victim; (2) the bully has an intent to harm, knowing he or she will inflict emotional or physical pain, and revels in that fact; (3) a threat of further aggression exists, in which the bully and victim both know that this act of aggression will not be the last; and (4) terror persists—the extreme, continuing agitation of the victim. The essence of bullying, according to Coloroso, is not anger but contempt. The bully sees the bullied as not worth respect or empathy. The bully is consummately arrogant.

Bullying and Violence

In July 2003, James Lovett, a recent high school graduate from the suburbs of Philadelphia, and two teenage companions were arrested after a failed carjacking attempt. Authorities subsequently found the trio had amassed a cache of weapons, including guns and swords, along with notes in which James threatened to avenge the wrongs of the world. Lovett had been a loner in school. One of his classmates said everyone "picked on" James.

Many psychologists and educators see a real connection between this kind of bullying and subsequent violence, and law enforcement agencies have linked bullying to the rise of violence in schools. In the wake of the Columbine High School shootings, the Federal Bureau of Investigation's (FBI) Critical Response Group of the National Center for the Analysis of Violent Crime studied 18 schools around the country. Thirteen were high schools and three were middle schools; all but one were public schools. Fourteen of the 18 schools studied had experienced actual school shootings. Although the investigators acknowledged that "the origins of human violence are complex," they found that schools where bullying is part of the school culture are more likely to be the targets of school shooters. The Critical Response Group also identified personality traits and behaviors of school shooters that are chillingly characteristic of school bullies or their victims, including poor coping skills, lack of resiliency, alienation, dehumanization of others, lack of empathy, intolerance, exaggerated sense of entitlement, low sense of esteem, and anger management problems (O'Toole, 2000).

Perhaps even more alarming is the result of a five-year retrospective study by researchers from the U.S. Centers for Disease Control and Prevention's Division of Violence Prevention on school-associated violent deaths, which directly linked victims of bullying with future aggressive behavior that resulted in school homicides. The research team investigated hundreds of student deaths occurring at or near schools from July 1, 1994, through June 30, 1999. The team identified students who had been bullied by their peers as a particularly high-risk population, prone to retaliate to the bullying in an aggressive manner.

The school shootings of the 1990s were a call to alarm that shocked the educational community and general public. Many schools and districts installed metal detectors or instituted zero tolerance policies to deal with student violence. More proactive schools implemented bullying prevention or antibullying programs. However, the *Indicators of School Crime and Safety: 2003* report from the National Center for Educational Statistics and the Bureau of Justice Statistics shows that, overall, while incidents of school violence have decreased in the last several years, reported incidents of bullying behaviors have increased (DeVoe et al,. 2003). Data from a nationally representative sample of students suggest that at least one out of every eight students in U.S. schools has been bullied on more than one occasion. One out of every three students in grades 6 through 10 reports being involved in bullying in some way, as perpetrator, victim, or both (Nansel et al., 2001). This is the *new* call to alarm to which this book seeks to respond.

Distinguishing Bullying, Harassment, and Threats

Bullying is not a legal term. Bullying is often not recognized for what it is and is often passed off as mere teasing or kidding around, a "normal" part of growing up. When confronted, bullies may assert the right to freedom of speech, the right to say what they want, to whom they want. School authorities often look the other way when bullying occurs because they do not know how to react, or they fear that calling attention to the situation may make it even worse. Several states have taken action by passing laws that make bullying illegal. However, unless a specific state statute exists, bullying, in and of itself, is not legally recognized as a cause of action for civil damages or as a criminal activity. When bullying escalates to harassment or is recognized as harassment, both federal and state laws may pertain. When bullying becomes a true threat, both federal and state laws also may apply. Both civil and criminal penalties may attach to legally cognizable harassment or threats.

The line between "mere bullying" and harassment that is recognized under the law is often a fine one. Courts, on more than one occasion, have admonished plaintiffs that "simple teasing" and name-calling are not illegal and may even be protected by the First Amendment. However, in addition to a verbal component, harassment frequently includes conduct, which is not protected by the First Amendment.

Harassment, although it may involve words, also involves conduct. Harassment can even escalate to stalking. Whether in person or remote, as when it is accomplished by mail or by communications technology, harassment is legally cognizable. Educators and entire districts may be held liable for not dealing with harassment in the school setting. Threats carry the same significance. Again, educators need to be prepared to recognize and deal with harassment and threats in appropriate ways.

Educators at all levels, from classroom to school-board room, must be aware of what the law says about bullying, harassment, and threats and how courts will view causes of action brought by victims. Will schools and school districts be held liable for the actions of students who bully, harass, or threaten other students? What are the responsibilities of school administrators and other school personnel when they witness or are made aware of bullying, harassment, or threats?

Bullying is not necessarily harassment, and a threat is not necessarily a true threat under the law. However, the distinctions may be subtle. Administrators and other school personnel may be called upon to act reflexively in many situations, without benefit of legal counsel. All educators must know how to recognize bullying and to distinguish bullying from childish teasing or from more serious persecution. Words do hurt. Conduct, of course, can hurt both emotionally and physically. Educators have to be ready to intervene and stop those hurts when it is appropriate to do so, without making the school environment a totalitarian state where no student expressive activity is tolerated. The purpose of this book is to help educators do this.

Chapter 1 begins by setting out general legal principles that determine how courts handle lawsuits alleging that school districts, school officials, or school personnel have tolerated or supported bullying, harassment, or threats in the school setting. Subsequent chapters treat specific legal implications of and legal responses to allegations of bullying in schools; harassment of students by teachers, peers, and other school personnel; harassment of teachers; and student threats in the school setting. Finally, a comprehensive chapter on recommendations for educators summarizes the actions that districts and individuals are undertaking to prevent and deal with bullying, harassment, and threats in the school setting.

Annotated References and Resources

Journal Articles, Texts, and Commentaries

• Professor Dan Olweus of the University of Bergen, Norway, published the first research studies linking bullying behavior to later criminal activity. Although accessibility to Olweus' early reports is limited by language (Olweus wrote in Norwegian and published in Scandinavian journals), he later reported his data in several books published in English. See, for example, Olweus, D. (1993) *Bullying at school: What we know and what we can do.* Cambridge: Blackwell.

In addition, Olweus' data has been widely accepted, corroborated, and disseminated in myriad publications and on many Web sites dealing with bullying and its prevention, among them the following:

– Glassey, D. S. (2001). Protecting our children. Washington, DC: The National Association of Attorneys Generals. Accessed April 2004 at www.naag.org/features/bullying.php
– Ericson, N. (2001, June). Addressing the problem of juvenile bullying. *OJJDP Fact Sheet 27.* (FS-200127) Washington, DC: The U.S. Department of Justice, Office of Juvenile Justice and Delinquency. Accessed April 2004 at http://ojjdp.ncjrs.org/publications/PubAbstract.asp?pubi=5823
– Wierner, J. (2001, June 26). *Congressional Children's Caucus briefing on bullying.* American Academy of Child and Adolescent Psychiatry Report presented to the Congressional Children's Caucus. [Wiener cites statistics from the National Institute on

Child Health and Human Development corroborating Olweus' data]. Accessed April 2004 as a PDF file at www.aacap.org/legislation/PDFs/bullying601.PDF
– Fox, J. A., Elliot, D. S., Kerlikowske, R. G., Newman, S. A., & Christeson, W. (2003). *Bullying prevention is crime prevention.* Washington, DC: Fight Crime: Invest in Kids. Accessed April 2004 at www.fightcrime.org

• The National Center for Injury Prevention and Control's Fact Sheet on Youth Violence listing "bullying other children or being the target of bullies" as a risk factor for youth violence is available at www.cdc.gov/ncipc/factsheets/yvfacts.htm (accessed April 2004).

• The report of the National Institute of Child Health and Human Development (NICHD) demonstrating a strong and consistent relationship between bullying and subsequent violent behaviors among U.S. children is Nansel, T. R., Overpeck, M. D., Haynie, D. L., Ruan, J., & Scheidt, P. C. (2003). Relationships between bullying and violence among U.S. youth. *Archives of Pediatric and Adolescent Medicine, 157*(4), 348–353. The report is available with a subscription at www.archpediatrics.com (accessed April 2004).

• Barbara Coloroso identifies four elements that characterize bullies in Coloroso, B. (2003). *The bully, the bullied, and the bystander: From preschool to high school–How parents can break the cycle of violence.* New York: HarperCollins.

• The report of the FBI's Critical Response Group is O'Toole, M. E. (2000). *The school shooter: A threat assessment perspective.* Washington, DC: Federal Bureau of Investigation. Accessed April 2004 as a .PDF file at www.fbi.gov/publications.htm

• The five-year retrospective study by researchers from the U.S. Centers for Disease Control and Prevention's Division of Violence Prevention on school-associated violent deaths was reported in the *Journal of the American Medical Association (JAMA)*. See Anderson, M., Kaufman, J., Simon, T. R., Barrios, L., Paulozzi, L., Ryan, G., Hammond, R., et al. (2001). School-associated violent deaths in the United States, 1994-1999. *Journal of the American Medical Association, 286,* 2695–2701. The researchers also report that at least one out of every eight students in U.S. schools has been bullied on more than one occasion. The researchers' article is available as a PDF file at www.cdc.gov/ncipc/pub-res/pubs.htm (accessed April 2004).

• DeVoe, J. F., Peter, K., Kaufman, P., Ruddy, S. A., Miller, A. K., Planty, M., Synder, T. D., et al (2003, October). *Indicators of school crime and safety: 2003.* Washington, DC: National Center for Educational Statistics and the Bureau of Justice Statistics. The Executive Summary from the report is available at www.nces.ed.gov/edstats/. The report indicates that the victimization crime rate in schools dropped from 48 per 1000 students in 1992 to 28 per 1000 students in 2001. See www.nces.ed.gov/pubs2004/crime03/index.asp (accessed April 2004).

• Another *JAMA* article reports that one out of every three students in grades 6–10 are involved in bullying in some way. See Nansel, T. R., Overpeck, M., Pilla, R. S., Ruan, W. J., & Simons-Morton, B. G. (2001). Bullying behaviors among the US youth: Prevalence and association with psychosocial adjustment. *Journal of the American Medical Association, 285,* 2131–2132.

CHAPTER ONE

Necessary Legal Background

THE U.S. LEGAL SYSTEM SHARES MANY FEATURES WITH THE SCIENCE OF geology. According to geologists, new rocks are laid down over the old in a continual process of building. Newer rocks may command more immediate attention, but the old rocks are still there, deeper but providing a foundation for the new. The process of accretion of new material over old resembles the growth of the law. New decisions are continually added to the body of the old, but the old law still remains as foundation. In legal terminology, this is the principle of *stare decisis*. New court decisions and laws continually build upon and add to the older body of law, but the old decisions remain and become the substratum on which the newer decisions stand. More recent decisions must be based on the precedents established by prior court decisions.

Rock formations, like legal decisions, can extend over large expanses of territory, or they can be local and unique. This situation is analogous to the legal principle of *controlling authority*. Subsequent court decisions cannot contradict prior decisions that are controlling in its jurisdictional area, except on the rare occasions where a court declares that *its own* former ruling is no longer good law. Said another way, not every court decision has the power to influence subsequent decisions in every locality. Some decisions apply only locally; others are more geographically widespread in their applicability. For example, a Pennsylvania Commonwealth Court ruling that a certain school district in Chester County,

Pennsylvania, may legally require students to wear school uniforms applies only in that district and is not controlling authority statewide or in other states. A court ruling from the federal district court for the Eastern District of Pennsylvania, on the other hand, is controlling authority for court decisions in the eastern part of Pennsylvania, and it may be persuasive authority in other parts of Pennsylvania or in nearby states. Similarly, a court decision handed down in the Third Circuit Court of Appeals is controlling authority for court deliberations in all the states of the Third Circuit: Pennsylvania, New Jersey, and Delaware. States in the Third Circuit must decide cases in conformity with the rulings of the Third Circuit Court of Appeals. Courts in other states with similar demographics, when faced with similar factual circumstances, may find a particular Third Circuit decision persuasive and may defer to it by ruling in accordance with it, but they are not legally bound to do so.

Continuing with the geologic analogy, geologists observe that every now and then a volcanic eruption occurs and completely covers the landscape with new, and perhaps foreign, rock. This is the geological counterpart of a Supreme Court decision. When the volcano that is the Supreme Court belches forth a decision, the law of the land changes. However, like a volcano, the Supreme Court cannot erupt at will. Pressure for the eruption must build. The Court must wait until circumstances present to it a case that is ripe for decision, and the decision it renders must address only the question presented. In a sense, the new rock laid down by a Supreme Court decision covers only certain streaks of existing rock. The other rock, not covered by the Court decision, remains *stare decisis*, and it may be controlling or merely persuasive authority, depending on its origin and geographic applicability.

Other details of the U.S. legal system defy analogy with tenets of geology or any other discipline, which is why law schools proliferate and prosper. Law students must learn

• Precepts of common law, the heritage of the United States' former status as a colony of Great Britain;

• Peculiarities of state constitutions and laws, under which states can, because of their own unique 17th- and 18th-century origins as autonomous civic entities, give more protections to their citizens than the U.S. Constitution bestows; and, of course,

• Details of federal constitutional law and federal statutes.

Purpose and Goal of the Book

Educators alone cannot negotiate the slopes and crevasses of the multifaceted mountain that is U.S. jurisprudence. In assessing the legal implications of school bullying and harassment, as in many aspects of what educators must contend with on a daily basis, legal counsel is critical. However, neither school administrators nor teachers typically have lawyers resident in their offices or classrooms. Many school situations require an immediate and specific response. District counsel is not always available when potentially explosive situations arise and immediate action is required. Educators need to know how to administer "first aid" in such situations. That is the purpose and goal of this book: to present, in language readily understandable to administrators, teachers, and other school personnel, basic information about the legal issues surrounding school bullying, harassment in the school setting, and student threats; and to provide practical and specific recommendations for both short- and long-term responses the school community must undertake. The book also attempts to provide, as "Annotated References and Resources" at the end of each chapter, specific references to court decisions and statutes that will enable school attorneys or other interested members of the educational community to research primary sources.

Just as educators have many legal authorities, statutes, and precedents to take into account when reacting to instances of harassment in the school setting, so the alleged victims of school-related bullying or harassment have many avenues of recourse. The most problematic of these for educators may be an alleged victim's resorting to litigation, either as a first response or when all other avenues for redress have failed. In situations in which harm is either perceived or real, aggrieved parties may follow the school district's prescribed avenues for filing complaints or appeal to agencies charged with enforcing victims' rights statutes (e.g., the Department of Justice, the Office for Civil Rights, or the state or federal Department of Education). Factual situations and prior dealings with schools often determine the paths students, parents, or other affected parties select, but the failure of educators nearest to the problem to address controllable situations exacerbates both the issues and the actions taken by those who feel victimized.

Issues in Litigation

Individuals who seek redress of perceived injuries through the court system have relatively few initial hurdles. Lawyers are readily available to handle cases for plaintiffs, even on a contingency fee basis, especially if potential lawsuits include recovery of substantial monetary damages or attorneys' fees. Individuals may also be representative of an entire class of victims, making a class action suit a possibility, with the concomitant return of even greater monetary reward for damages, in which the lawyer can share.

Except for cases of fraud where allegations of wrongdoing must be pleaded with particular attention to detail, court rules in civil cases allow for *notice pleading*. Notice pleading allows alleged victims to bring suit in court before all the facts are known, relying on depositions and other methods of investigation and discovery to uncover the details of the defendant's wrongdoing. In criminal lawsuits the state actually brings the charges on behalf of the plaintiff.

Legal strategy is important for both the alleged victim and the defendant, whether individual, representative of a class, public official, or school board. The alleged wrong or asserted statutory violation determines the standard of review the court will apply. The standard of review, in turn, often determines the outcome of the case. For example, if a plaintiff alleges deprivation of a constitutional right by the government or government official, the court will apply the strictest standard of review. The government will have to show that its actions served a compelling state interest and were narrowly tailored to achieve its goal in a manner that least impacted individual freedom. On the other hand, if the alleged governmental deprivation does not concern a constitutionally protected interest, the standard of review may be less stringent. The government will be required to demonstrate a rational reason for the limitation of the individual's freedom, but a rational reason is easier to justify than a compelling reason. Standards of review intermediate between these two extremes also exist. In all cases, the standard of review a court applies influences the outcome of the decision.

Causes of Action

If a bullied, harassed, or threatened student or school employee seeks relief through litigation in the courts, several approaches are possible, and they are not mutually exclusive. The student (through her parents or caregivers) or the employee may assert one or more causes of action in one lawsuit. Injured parties may sue school districts or individuals within the district in their personal as well as official capacities, or all three simultaneously. Causes of action can include both civil and criminal suits alleging violations of constitutional rights, both state and federal; violations of rights guaranteed by state or federal statutes; or violations of common law duties, as when an aggrieved party alleges a tort such as negligence or intentional infliction of emotional distress.

School districts are entities constituted by the state. Therefore, school officials and educators within a school district are state actors, against whom the prohibitions of the Bill of Rights operate. State actors cannot deprive either students or school personnel of basic rights guaranteed by the U.S. Constitution. If they do, the affected party can bring a suit alleging violation of a federal constitutional right. However, a constitutional cause of action can serve as either a sword or a shield. The victim of harassment or threats at the hands of school personnel may allege violations of the Fourth Amendment guarantee against forcible governmental seizure. A school bully or harasser, on the other hand, may defend her actions as speech or expressive conduct that merits protection as "pure speech" under the First Amendment. The First Amendment guarantees that speech and expression be free of governmental restraint.

The alleged harasser may also assert violation of her rights to due process and equal protection under the Fourteenth Amendment. The right to due process means that before disciplinary action is taken against a student, the student must be given notice of the charges against her and provided an opportunity to respond. Generally, the more serious the discipline involved, the more extensive are the student's due process rights. In cases of minor infractions meriting relatively minor discipline, an informal hearing in the principal's office, with an opportunity for the student to tell her side of the story, may be all that is required. However, in cases where suspension or expulsion is contemplated, school districts must afford students more formal proceedings; in some cases, these include the opportunity to call witnesses, have legal counsel present, and appeal in cases of adverse decisions.

In conjunction with a Fourteenth Amendment claim, the victim of harassment or threats may also assert that her civil rights have been violated. Several federal statutes prohibit discrimination that would violate an individual's civil rights. One such statute is Section

1983 of Title 42 of the United States Code. Originally enacted by Congress as part of the Ku Klux Klan Act and also known as the Civil Rights Act of 1871, Section 1983 was designed to provide a means for freed slaves to enforce the equal protection guarantees of the Fourteenth Amendment and to protect against infringement of their constitutional rights by state officials. To succeed in a Section 1983 claim, a plaintiff must show that the alleged violation of civil rights occurred "under color of state law," that is, at the hand of a state actor; and that the alleged violation deprived the plaintiff of rights guaranteed by the U.S. Constitution or by a federal statute. Section 1983 is frequently appended as a cause of action in school-related lawsuits because it provides for payment of attorneys' fees by the non-prevailing party in certain egregious cases.

Several other federal antidiscrimination laws provide protections based on different civil rights and may serve as causes of action for plaintiffs deprived of educational benefits. Title VI of the Civil Rights Act of 1964 provides protection against discrimination based on race, religion, or ethnic background in programs or activities receiving federal financial assistance. Although recent court decisions suggest that individuals can bring suit under Title VI only for intentional discrimination, complaints that an educational program or activity has a discriminatory effect, even if unintentional, can be made to the Office for Civil Rights which investigates and reports violations to the Department of Justice.

Title VII, which prohibits discrimination in the workplace, is also a part of the Civil Rights Act of 1964. Teachers and other paid school district employees may bring suit under Title VII if they suffer adverse employment actions because of their race, color, religion, sex, or national origin.

Often recognized as modeled on Title VI, Title IX, part of the Education Amendments of 1972, prohibits discrimination based on sex in educational programs or activities receiving federal funds.

Although Title IX is most familiar to the public in the context of parity of school athletic programs for men and women, its stated purpose was to encourage women to participate in intellectually demanding programs of study on an equal footing with men. Individuals may bring an action in court if educational benefits or opportunities are denied on account of sex, or if gender-based harassment causes deprivation of educational opportunities or benefits.

Other federal laws provide protections against discrimination based on disabilities or handicaps, even though they did not originate as civil rights statutes or are not exclusively addressed to the educational setting. Moreover, state constitutions and state laws often parallel these federal protections or even provide more expansive protections to alleged victims. Subsequent chapters will address these issues in more detail.

Besides violations of constitutional rights or rights guaranteed by specific statutes, aggrieved parties may bring causes of action under common law theories. Negligence is a tort, or civil cause of action, that originates in the common law. Four elements must be present in asserting a cause of action for negligence. First, there must be a duty. For example, an aggrieved party can assert that school officials have a duty of caring for students. Next, that duty must be breached. Third, the breach of the duty must be the cause of the injury asserted. Finally, quantifiable damage must occur as a result of the breach. Victims of bullying may assert negligence on the part of school personnel but may not be able to quantify damages. Bullying or harassment that originated in school may occur and escalate outside school. Courts generally will not hold school districts responsible for actions over which the school has no direct authority.

Defenses to Litigation

In addition, school officials and school districts often may assert affirmative defenses to many causes of action raised in litigation. Even if a school official or school employee has been negligent, the district itself may argue that it should not be held liable for the actions of its employees under the theory of sovereign immunity. The defense of sovereign immunity is based on the premise that allowing individuals to sue and recover monetary damages from governmental entities would divert public monies to the good of only a few and deplete the state treasury. Such depletion of funds would disadvantage the general public, whose taxes support public education.

Although sovereign immunity is a defense available to school districts as entities, school officials sued in their personal capacities may assert a different defense: the defense of qualified immunity. Qualified immunity, in a nutshell, is available if a doubt exists about whether the school official's action was actually illegal. For example, a teacher who disciplined an unruly student by duct-taping him to his chair may assert qualified immunity because such punishment is not prohibited in the teacher's district. However, once it is established that duct taping is a prohibited corporal punishment in that district, the defense of qualified immunity is not available. The essence of qualified immunity is that while ignorance of the law is never an excuse, in some cases, absence of a law may be.

Motions to Dismiss

For better or for worse, many plaintiffs who bring causes of action against school districts or school employees never get their day in court. Many court cases are resolved even before actual evidence is presented because they do not survive motions to dismiss made by defendants. Just about anyone can allege a cause of action for just about any perceived injury against just about any school district or school employee. The only requirement is that the injury be presented properly before the court. However, courts have limited time and limited resources; mechanisms must be in place to resolve frivolous or unfounded lawsuits expeditiously. Hence, the availability of the motion to dismiss.

Immediately after the plaintiff files suit, before any evidence is presented by either party to the suit, the defendant may move to dismiss the suit. The court then decides, on its own, whether there is any legal theory under which the cause of action presented can survive. If the court rules that there is not, the court grants the motion to dismiss, and the lawsuit ends there. The plaintiff, unhappily, has lost her lawsuit before it even really began. Rulings on motions to dismiss can then deter other plaintiffs from bringing similar causes of action.

The applicable standard of review for a defendant's motion to dismiss is that a court may grant the motion only if it appears beyond doubt that the plaintiff has no legal argument that would support a decision in her favor. The court must examine the facts stated in the plaintiff's complaint, and decide, giving the plaintiff every benefit of the doubt, whether the "wrong" described by the plaintiff is recognized as a violation of a legal right. Granting a motion to dismiss ends a lawsuit before it officially begins.

In some cases, however, the court refuses to dismiss the suit. This action may encourage the parties to reach an out-of-court settlement. Refusals to dismiss also have significance; they signal the plaintiff that similar causes of action will likely be recognized as viable causes of action.

Sometimes cases cannot be decided until both sides present evidence for the court to consider. In this case, depositions are taken and witnesses are lined up. After the evidence is collected, either side or both sides may feel that their evidence is so compelling that a decision in their favor is inevitable. One or both parties may then move for summary judgment. In deciding a motion for summary judgment, the judge must consider all the evidence in the light most favorable to the moving party and issue a ruling based solely on the applicable law. If the judge rules in the defendant's favor, the lawsuit stops there and all parties go home. If, however, the judge rules in the plaintiff's favor, the lawsuit may continue, or, in many cases, the defendant will negotiate a settlement with the plaintiff.

Motions to dismiss and motions for summary judgment are very important in defining the legal landscape in cases involving bullying, harassment, and threats in the school setting. When a motion to dismiss or a motion for summary judgment is granted in favor of the plaintiff and a settlement follows, the public will often never ascertain the ultimate disposition of the case, because the court can seal the settlement record. All the public will know is which party the court ruled had the better case. However, lawyers for both plaintiffs and defendants pay close attention to such rulings.

Controlling or Persuasive Authority

The authority of the courts to adjudicate educational disputes derives from Article III of the U.S. Constitution, which created the Supreme Court and a series of lesser courts to decide controversies involving the states and the citizens of the United States. The power of the courts to adjudicate disputes is called judicial review, a review that ordinarily proceeds in an orderly fashion from lower levels of the various court systems to higher levels, as needed.

The two court systems that handle most school-related controversies are the more or less parallel systems of the state and federal courts. As a general rule, the plaintiff chooses the forum in which to litigate a dispute, if school and administrative remedies are exhausted and judicial review is therefore appropriate. State courts are available for any individuals seeking redress of wrongs having a legally cognizable nexus to that state. To bring suit in federal court, on the other hand, a plaintiff must show that a federal question is involved. This is relatively easy to accomplish in the educational setting because the federal government provides financial assistance to state educational systems, constitutional issues are federal questions, and any dispute involving a federal law is a federal question.

When a court renders a decision, however, the force and applicability of that decision depends on the status of the court in the hierarchy of the state or federal court system. As in the geology analogy, Supreme Court decisions blanket the legal landscape like the lava from a volcanic eruption. Decisions of the Supreme Court become the law of the land, and decisions in all inferior courts, both state and federal systems, must accord with the Supreme Court's decision, unless the Court itself renders its decision null and void in a subsequent ruling.

In the federal court system, the intermediate courts just below the Supreme Court are the various federal Circuit Courts of Appeals. The United States and its territories are divided into 13 circuits based predominantly on geographical proximity. Parties dissatisfied with rulings in federal district courts may appeal to the Circuit Courts of Appeals. Decisions in the Courts of Appeals are controlling authority for all lower, or federal district courts, in their respective jurisdictions. However, a decision in one circuit court is not controlling authority for other circuit court decisions. If the circuits are geographically, economically, or demographically similar, however, decisions in sister circuits may be persuasive and influence the outcome of rulings on common topics. On some topics, for example, on the topic of what constitutes a true student threat, rulings in the various circuits differ fundamentally, with several circuits adopting a test that relies on the interpretation of the hearer, and others adopting a test that focuses on what the speaker should have realized about the impact of his words. In cases where splits of legal opinions exist among the circuit courts, the Supreme Court will often agree to hear the appeal of a case or cases that will allow them to resolve the legal uncertainty. However, appeals to the

Supreme Court are not automatically granted. The Court accepts only a limited number of cases for adjudication each year.

Paralleling the federal court system is an extensive system of state courts through which plaintiffs may seek relief. As in the federal system, state courts operate on a hierarchy system, with appeals from courts of localized jurisdiction to courts of more regional jurisdiction. Each state typically has one state Supreme Court that is the highest court in the state system, except for New York, where the highest state court is the Court of Appeals. Decisions of a state Supreme Court are binding on lower courts in that state, but they are not controlling authority for courts in other states. Other states, however, are bound to recognize the outcome of state court decisions, for example, divorce decrees. State Supreme Court decisions can be appealed to the United States Supreme Court if a federal question is at issue.

Interpreting Case Citations

Understanding the court and legal citations is imperative to determine if a particular case or law is binding for a school or district. The citation rules used by the legal profession are different from, and in most cases use more abbreviations than, the rules formulated by nonlegal scholars. Court decisions are reported in upper- and lower-case letters. The names of plaintiffs and defendants (or in appeals cases, appellants and appellees) appear first, and are either underlined or italicized. "Versus" is abbreviated simply as "v.," not "vs."

The rest of the citation provides the information needed to find the text of the decision. Court cases are usually collected in what are called *reporters*, which can be local, state, federal, or topical. Geographic reporters collect cases originating in different jurisdictions, whereas specialty reporters collect cases dealing with particular topics. For example, the *Atlantic Reporter*, abbreviated "A.," contains cases from Pennsylvania, New Jersey, and several neighboring states.

West's *Education Law Reporter*, abbreviated "Ed. Law Rep.," reprints court decisions having special significance for educators and school attorneys. Several reporters are exclusively dedicated to decisions from the federal courts, such as the *Federal Reporter*, abbreviated "F.," or the *Federal Supplement*, abbreviated "F. Supp."

The reporters publish court decisions as they are decided, so the most recent cases appear in the most recent reporters. The first number of a case citation gives the reporter volume; the number after the reporter's abbreviation is the page on which the case begins. As decision after decision was published, the volume numbers of the reporters got higher and higher. Someone eventually said, "Enough!" and started the numbering all over again. To keep things straight, new reporters were designated as "the Second" and eventually even "the Third" series of the given reporter. In keeping with the law's citation brevity, the Second series is designated "2d," and the Third "3d." There are even corresponding rules about how many spaces are allowed between number and reporter abbreviations.

The final part of the case citation identifies the court that decided the case and the year of the decision. For example, the court might be a state court in the Eastern District of Pennsylvania from 1997. The citation would include the following information in parentheses:

(E.D. Pa. 1997)

Or the decision may be from a state appeals court in California, dated 1999. The citation then would be:

(Cal. App. 1999)

If just "Cal." appears, the case is from the California Supreme Court. Similarly, any other state abbreviation indicates that the decision originated in that state's Supreme Court (except for New York State, where the New York Supreme Court is *not* the highest court in the state. The state court of last resort in New York is the Court of Appeals).

If the decision originated in a federal Circuit Court of Appeals instead of the state system, the part of the citation in parentheses indicates the specific circuit where the case was decided. For example, a decision from the federal Circuit Court of Appeals in which California is located—the Ninth Circuit—would be designated as such:

(9th Cir. 1999)

The decisions with the most universal applicability—those from the U.S. Supreme Court—are the easiest to cite and to recognize. U.S. Supreme Court decisions appear in several reporters, among them the *United States Reporter*, abbreviated "U.S.," or the *Supreme Court Reporter*, abbreviated "S. Ct." An example of a Supreme Court case citation is *Brown v. Board of Education,* 347 U.S. 483 (1954).

Some decisions are rendered by courts but are not reported in official reporters. Such "unreported decisions" are legally binding on the parties, but they do not have precedential value. Courts are not obligated to decide subsequent cases in accord with them. However, unreported decisions are made public. Many appear online, in the press, or cited in law reviews or other legal publications. Unreported decisions may state persuasive arguments that influence subsequent deliberations.

Annotated References and Resources

Constitutional and Statutory References

• The First Amendment to the U.S. Constitution provides that "Congress shall make no law respecting the establishment of religion, or prohibiting the free exercise thereof; or abridging the freedom of speech, or of the press; or the right of the people peaceably to assemble, and to petition the Government for a redress of grievances."

• The Fourth Amendment provides that "The right of the people to be secure in their persons, houses, papers, and effects, against unreasonable searches and seizures, shall not be violated, and no Warrants shall issue, but upon probable cause, supported by Oath or affirmation, and particularly describing the place to be searched, and the persons or things to be seized."

• Section 1 of the Fourteenth Amendment, containing the due process and equal protection clauses, provides that "All persons born or naturalized in the United States, and subject to the jurisdiction thereof, are citizens of the United States and of the State wherein they reside. No State shall make or enforce any law which shall abridge the privileges or immunities of citizens of the United States; nor shall any State deprive any person of life, liberty, or property, without due process of law; nor deny to any person within its jurisdiction the equal protection of the laws."

• Known as Section 1983, 42 U.S.C. § 1983 of the Civil Rights Act of 1871 states:

> Every person who, under color of any statute, ordinance, regulation, custom, or usage, of any State or Territory or the District of Columbia, subjects or causes to be subjected, any citizen of the United States or other person within the jurisdic-

tion thereof to the deprivation of any rights, privileges, or immunities secured by the Constitution and laws, shall be liable to the party injured in an action at law, suit in equity, or other proper proceeding for redress . . . .

In other words, Section 1983 provides a remedy for violations of constitutional rights or rights under federal law. To state a cognizable claim under Section 1983, a plaintiff must allege that the conduct of a person acting under color of state law caused the violation, at least in part, and that the conduct deprived the plaintiff of a right secured by the Constitution or by laws of the United States. School districts and school boards are local government entities that can be held liable under Section 1983, but only if they establish an official policy, or tolerate a custom or practice, that leads to, causes, or results in the deprivation of a constitutionally protected right. (*Monell v. Department of Social Services,* 436 U.S. 58 (1978)). The "toleration" can be inaction in the face of repeated notification of problems, as in *Massey v. Akron City Board of Education,* 82 F. Supp.2d 735 (N.D. Ohio, 2000). Public school district employees such as administrators and teachers, as state actors, can be personally liable for violations under Section 1983.

• Title VI of the Civil Rights Act of 1964, 42 U.S.C. § 2000 c, d, provides that "[n]o person in the United States shall, on the ground of race, color, or national origin, be excluded from participation in, be denied the benefits of, or be subjected to discrimination under any program or activity receiving Federal financial assistance." The court decision foreclosing private rights of action under Title VI, except in cases of intentional discrimination, is *Alexander v. Sandoval,* 121 S. Ct. 1511 (2001).

• Title VII of the Civil Rights Act of 1964, as amended, 42 U.S.C. § 2000 e – 2 (a) (1), prohibits discrimination "against any individual with respect to his compensation, terms, conditions, or privileges of employment, because of such individual's race, color, religion, sex, or national origin."

• Title IX of the Education Amendments of 1972, 20 U.S.C. § 1681, provides that "[n]o person . . . shall on the basis of sex, be excluded from participation in, be denied the benefits of, or be subjected to discrimination under any educational program or activity receiving Federal financial assistance."

• The Americans with Disabilities Act of 1990 (ADA), 42 U.S.C.A. § 12101, prohibits discrimination in employment against any "qualified individual with a disability." Coverage is not dependent upon an employer's receipt of federal funds.

• Section 504 of the Rehabilitation Act of 1973, 29 U.S.C. § 794, provides that "no otherwise handicapped individual . . . shall, solely by reason of his handicap, be excluded from the participation in, or be denied the benefits of, or be subjected to discrimination under any program or activity receiving Federal financial assistance."

• The U.S. Courts of Appeals are intermediate appellate courts in the federal court system. Appeal from a federal district court is to one of the Courts of Appeals, and subsequently to the U.S. Supreme Court. There are thirteen federal appellate circuits, twelve of which have regional jurisdiction; and one that has jurisdiction in patent, copyright, and trademark cases. Eleven of the 12 regional circuits are numbered, and the states in each numbered region are listed below. The unnumbered District of Columbia Circuit handles appeals from the federal district court in the District of Columbia. Decisions in the numbered circuit courts are binding in the states in that regional circuit:

   – First Circuit: Maine, Massachusetts, New Hampshire, Rhode Island, and Puerto Rico

   – Second Circuit: Vermont, New York, and Connecticut

– Third Circuit: Pennsylvania, New Jersey, Delaware, and the Virgin Islands

– Fourth Circuit: Virginia, West Virginia, North Carolina, South Carolina, and Maryland

– Fifth Circuit: Texas, Mississippi, and Louisiana

– Sixth Circuit: Ohio, Kentucky, Tennessee, and Michigan

– Seventh Circuit: Indiana, Illinois, and Wisconsin

– Eighth Circuit: Minnesota, North Dakota, South Dakota, Missouri, Arkansas, Iowa, and Nebraska

– Ninth Circuit: Montana, Idaho, Washington, Oregon, California, Nevada, Arizona, Alaska, Hawaii, Guam, and the Northern Mariana Islands

– Tenth Circuit: Wyoming, Utah, Colorado, Oklahoma, New Mexico, and Kansas

– Eleventh Circuit: Alabama, Georgia, and Florida

Journal Articles, Texts, and Commentaries

• For a scholarly treatment of the origin and import of the Bill of Rights and the interplay between the Bill of Rights and the Fourteenth Amendment, see Amar, A.R. (1992). The Bill of Rights and the Fourteenth Amendment. *Yale Law Journal, 101.* 1193–1284. Amar's commentary is available at www.saf.org/LawReviews/Amar/html (accessed May 2004).

• For more detailed information on interpreting case citations and the applicability of court rulings to particular jurisdictions, see Chapter 1 in Conn, K. (2002). *The Internet and the law: What educators need to know.* Alexandria, VA: Association for Supervision and Curriculum Development.

CHAPTER TWO

School Bullies and Bullying

TEASING AND BEING TEASED ARE NORMAL PARTS OF GROWING UP. BULLYING is not. However, educators may be hard-pressed to differentiate between the two, and they may either overreact to normal teasing interactions between and among students or fail to react to incidents of true bullying, thereby giving tacit "permission" for the bullying to continue.

The essence of bullying is a power imbalance between the bully and victim. Whereas teasing is an interaction designed to provoke and may include elements of hostility, teasing occurs between children closely matched in size and physical ability. The teasing victim may even "pop" her tormentor, and tussles may result. The victim of bullying, on the other hand, feels powerless to retaliate; and if she finally takes action, homicide or suicide may be the outcome. Children who come from already unstable home situations may find bullying especially devastating.

Bullying harms both the victim and the bully. Bullies become at-risk for poor relationships later in life. Bullies are more likely than nonbullies to go on to become criminals and to end up in jail by the time they reach their twenties. The families of both victims and bullies become part of the problem, sharing the heartaches of the victim or suffering the carried-over aggression of the bully.

Recognizing Evidence of Bullying

Recognizing the signs that a child is being bullied is difficult, especially for educators preoccupied with the myriad frenzied duties imposed by public education today. Bullied students also tend to try to blend into the background, in the futile hope that their tormentor (or tormentors) will forget them or simply go away. Frequent stomachaches in school that require visits to the nurse, urination "accidents," frequent unexplained absences from school, poor concentration in school, unexplained irritability, inattention to schoolwork and unexplained failing grades, drug and alcohol abuse, self-mutilation or violence toward self or others—all may be warning signs of bullying, but they are also warning signs easily attributed to other causes, especially in middle school and junior high schools where most bullying occurs.

Not surprisingly, the medical community has expressed concern about the negative health and behavioral impacts of bullying, and has stressed the need for pediatricians to recognize and treat the symptoms of bullying. A pediatrician may be the first professional who has both the expertise and the opportunity to distinguish between symptoms of underlying medical pathology and bullying. Pediatrician James U. Scott and colleagues at the University of South Florida (2003) urge doctors to use strategies such as open-ended questions, empathetic encouragement, and even direct questions ("Do you have friends at school? Any enemies?") to get older children talking. The opportunity to draw with crayons or to interact with puppets during the course of physical examinations may help younger children express their feelings. Education professionals and parents may find the same or similar strategies useful.

Michael S. Jellinek (2003), chief of Child Psychiatry at Massachusetts General Hospital and a professor at Harvard Medical School in Boston, contends that bullying begins in preschool, when a toddler first yanks favorite toys away from weaker children. Parents should intervene, Jellinek asserts, but intervention does not mean spanking or other retaliatory violence that reinforces the idea of physical violence as a solution. Parents and teachers need to model appropriate social interactions. Parents who bully other family members with a dictatorial approach to decision making, or teachers who adopt domineering roles in the classroom, send a message that bullying is acceptable if one has the power to carry it off.

Bullying and the First Amendment

How do bullies "happen"? That is a question as complicated as the problem of recognizing and preventing bullying. Many adults, some educators among them, think that bullying is "all talk." They subscribe to the old adage, "Sticks and stones may break your bones, but words will never hurt you." Bullies, unfortunately, do use words. Insults and verbal intimidation are an important part of their repertoire, which is part of the problem of controlling bullying in schools.

Americans love to talk. Whether they talk in person, on telephones or cell phones, through e-mail or chat rooms, Americans consider freedom of expression one of their most basic rights and a defining characteristic of a free society. Students learn in elementary school that the First Amendment to the U.S. Constitution guarantees freedom of speech and expression. Many students think, then, that they are free to say whatever they want, whenever they feel the need, to whomever they decide needs to hear or experience their message.

However, public schools do not have to tolerate the speech or expression of bullies. If educators understand the scope and purpose of the First Amendment, and if they respond reasonably and appropriately to those who intimidate and harass others in the school setting, the law will be on their side.

What the First Amendment Protects

Very simply, the First Amendment guarantees only that the *federal government* will not interfere with or restrain the free expression of its citizens. The Bill of Rights as a whole, and the First Amendment in particular, reflects the Founding Fathers' distrust of the king of England and of all forms of centralized governmental power. The due process clause of the Fourteenth Amendment, ratified in 1868, extends the First Amendment guarantee of freedom of speech to protect all persons against interference or restraint of expression by *state governments* as well.

School personnel, as state actors, must respect the protections of the First Amendment. But the First Amendment shield is not absolute. Both federal and state governments, and even local governments acting under authority of the state, can set certain limits on certain types of expression in certain places, at certain times, and for certain reasons. Schools are one of those certain places. Administrators and teachers, as state actors, have power to restrict students' speech and expression above and beyond the restrictions that the government can place on adult speech. Moreover, even in the world outside schools and certainly in schools, some categories of speech are completely unprotected.

What the First Amendment Does *Not* Protect

Child Pornography. One of the most generally accepted categories of unprotected expression is child pornography. Producing, distributing, or simply possessing actual child pornography—that is, pornographic material that depicts real children performing sexually explicit acts—is not only unprotected expression, it is also a crime.

Two distinctions with regard to child pornography are legally significant. The first is that pornography involving adults or pornographic depictions of adults is not a crime. Adult pornography is distinguished from obscenity, which will be discussed, and is actually a protected form of expression under the First Amendment.

The second legally significant distinction is the difference between "actual" child pornography and what is called "virtual" child pornography: sexually explicit material that may appear to involve young children but was created using computer imagery or youthful-looking actors. Virtual child pornography is outside the purview of governmental restraints since the U.S. Supreme Court in 2002 struck down portions of the Child Pornography Prevention Act that would have made virtual child pornography a crime. Adults expressing themselves by masquerading as children in pornographic poses and computer images or animations of children engaged in pornographic acts, even though the material appears to be and is represented as child pornography, constitute protected expression.

That the Supreme Court drew the fine line between actual and virtual child pornography in deciding what kinds of expression the First Amendment protects demonstrates how reluctant the government is to suppress or chill personal expression. Despite this reluctance, however, four other categories of expression besides actual child pornography, all of which may emerge as elements of bullying or harassment, are also not protected by the First Amendment. One of these categories is obscene speech or expression.

Obscenity. What is obscenity, and how is it different from pornography? The Supreme Court in 1973 crafted a test, called the "*Miller* test," that defines obscenity as a description or depiction of

sexual conduct that, taken as a whole by an average person applying contemporary community standards, appeals to the prurient
interest and is patently offensive. In addition, the description or
depiction must lack serious literary, artistic, political, or scientific
value, as judged by a national rather than community standard.
Pornography, arguably, is less offensive expression that survives the
Miller test.

Courts have said that the prurient interest prong of the *Miller*
test implies a shameful or morbid kind of interest in sex, not merely
a lustful interest. What is not obscene for adults, however, may be
obscene for children, and the state can set a different standard for
obscenity in materials accessible to children. Federal, state, or local
governments may not prohibit the sale of sexually explicit material
to adults merely because it would be obscene for children.
Regulations may require that stores sell magazines or books
obscene for children in plain wrappers or that "adult stores" locate
away from school zones, but government cannot restrain material
merely because it is in bad taste.

Fighting Words and Clear and Present Dangers. Both
pornography and obscenity may be aspects of bullying or harassment that have sexual overtones. Two other categories of speech
unprotected by the First Amendment, "fighting words" and speech
or expression that creates a clear and present danger of imminent
lawless action, may also surface in bullying or harassment contexts
or constitute threats that are actionable under the law. An understanding of the legal meanings of the terms *fighting words* and *clear
and present danger* is essential for educators.

Fighting words are words or other kinds of expression that, by
their very nature, provoke a violent response from listeners. By their
very utterance or display, they inflict injury and incite lawless action.
The epithet "nigger" may be an example. Such an insult directed to
any person, whether a person of color or not, is calculated to

provoke a violent response. Displaying a white hood suggestive of Ku Klux Klan activities may also constitute fighting words in certain circumstances.

Speech or expression that presents a clear and present danger, on the other hand, involves a direct connection between its expression and violation of the law, or puts important governmental interests at risk. The clear and present danger doctrine has been applied to deny First Amendment protections to those who, in wartime, disclose intelligence information to the public. More relevant to the school setting, if a student posts in an Internet chat room explicit directions detailing how to hack into her school district's central computer system, such directions may arguably constitute a clear and present danger to the school, and at least one court has deemed such speech or personal expression outside the protection of the First Amendment.

Defamation. Defamatory speech or expression does not merit First Amendment protection. *Defamation* is untrue speech or written expression that injures a person's reputation or standing in the community. Also commonly called *slander* or *libel*, defamation exposes the victim of the untruth to ridicule, contempt, or hatred. Such expression causes others to stop associating with the subject of the defamatory remarks or lowers their esteem of her. The person publishing or disseminating defamatory remarks has malicious intent; that is, she knows that the information is false or recklessly disregards its truth or falsity. Spreading vicious gossip is a favorite tool of adolescent female bullies. Schools do not violate a student's right to free speech when suppressing defamatory gossip.

True Threats. Finally, the First Amendment does not protect speech or expression that fits the legal definition of true threats. A *true threat* under the law is an utterance or expressive act that is so "unequivocal, unconditional, immediate and specific" that it conveys a seriousness of purpose and the prospect of being carried out in the near future. Such expression serves no civic purpose, and schools are free to take disciplinary action against those who utter true threats in the school setting. However, as with all spoken communication, what the listener perceives and what the speaker intended may be two different messages. Deciding under the law whether a threat is a "true threat" is fraught with difficulty because the legal definition of a true threat is not uniformly applied. In some courts, the test is whether a reasonable speaker should have known that her words would be interpreted as a threat. In others, the test is whether a reasonable listener would perceive the words or expressive conduct as a true threat. A completely different level of complexity is whether anyone, speaker or listener, in the midst of a threatening confrontation, can make a reasonable decision.

The Power of Schools to Regulate Expression

Public schools do not have to tolerate the taunts of bullies, even those who assert the right of freedom of speech or expression, if school administrators and teachers are informed about the law. The First Amendment does not protect a bully's obscenities, fighting words, or insults that damage peers' relationships with other students. Teachers and administrators need to remember that, even though they are state actors and restrained by the First Amendment from suppressing protected speech, many of a bully's verbal tools fall outside the purview of the First Amendment. In fact, because schools are responsible for inculcating in students the values of civility and good citizenship, schools have even broader power and authority to restrict speech and expression than federal, state, or local governments. Moreover, elementary school personnel have the broadest power to regulate student speech, consistent with their responsibility to their younger students.

The courts have upheld the power of schools to regulate school-related student speech and expression, both inside and outside school. Three seminal decisions relating to student speech continue to shape First Amendment jurisprudence in the public school context. These are the familiar trilogy of decisions studied in all education law classes: *Tinker v. Des Moines Independent School District* (1969), *Bethel School District No. 403 v. Fraser* (1986), and *Hazelwood School District v. Kuhlmeier* (1988).

Brought to the courts' attention during the Vietnam War era, the *Tinker* controversy ultimately upheld the right of students to wear black armbands in school as a protest of the war. However, although the Supreme Court affirmed that "[i]t can hardly be argued that either students or teachers shed their constitutional rights to freedom of speech or expression at the schoolhouse gate," *Tinker* was not a paean for student self-expression. The Supreme Court explicitly acknowledged the special setting of the public schools with regard to the First Amendment and a school's need to prescribe and control conduct. Student expression that "materially disrupts classwork, or involves substantial disorder or invasion of the rights of others," the Court stated, "is not immunized by the constitutional guarantee" of the First Amendment. More simply put, a bully cannot assert the right to say whatever he wants because the First Amendment protects him, if school officials can show that his speech or expression is disrupting a class or interfering with the rights of other students.

Several years later, in *Bethel School District No. 403 v. Fraser*, the Supreme Court upheld the right of schools to censor student speech that did not rise to the level of obscenity but was merely lewd and vulgar. Stating that the rights of students in schools were not automatically as extensive as the rights of adults outside school, the Court upheld the Bethel School District's suspension of Matthew Fraser after Matthew delivered a sexually suggestive nominating speech for his friend at a school assembly.

Written student expression is also properly subject to censorship by school administrators if held out to the community as school-sponsored communication. The *Hazelwood* court upheld the right of a school administrator to delete controversial and objectionable articles from the school's newspaper because readers would reasonably view the school newspaper as bearing the imprimatur of the school. The principal's actions were, the Court said, related to legitimate pedagogical concerns.

Limits on School Regulation of Student Expression

Tinker, *Fraser*, and *Hazelwood* give schools wide latitude in regulating offensive or objectionable expression in schools. However, that latitude does have bounds, and recent court deliberations have tested and refined the parameters. Even in *Tinker*, the Court was careful to caution schools that they could not limit student expression merely because of some undifferentiated fear of disturbance. Before curtailing student expression, a school must demonstrate a concrete and particularized basis for their premonition of disruption. For example, a school could not ban the wearing of T-shirts bearing the image of the Confederate flag if race had never been an issue at the school. However, if racial tensions in the school were elevated, school administrators could allege a particularized and reasonable fear that allowing students to express themselves by wearing shirts emblazoned with the Confederate flag would further inflame an already tense situation and provoke substantial disturbance. Restraining students from displaying obvious and unmistakable gang emblems, or from distributing hate literature, for fear of their causing disruption in the school, would likewise seem constitutionally defensible.

Administrators and teachers must ascertain the tenor of court decisions throughout the judicial system as school-related First Amendment cases are decided. The courts have given school administrators and teachers latitude to curb the speech and expression of school bullies, so that all students can feel safe enough to learn what schools have to teach. Many courts have also upheld school districts' right to discipline students for out-of-school speech that negatively impacts, even indirectly, the orderly operation of schools. From cases involving students who hurl epithets at teachers in a shopping center parking lot to students who post offensive comments about teachers and peers on Web sites, courts are acknowledging that even out-of-school speech can cause material and substantial disruption in schools; they are upholding the rights of school districts to take action against such student expression (see also Walsh, 2003). Students' rights to freedom of speech and expression do not stop at the schoolhouse gate, but neither does bullying nor harassment.

The Internet and Bullying

The First Amendment also protects student speech and expression in cyberspace. When students create Web sites, post Internet "blogs," or contribute to chat room conversation outside school using privately owned computers or other technology resources, their expression often implicates school-related issues and revolves around their interactions with peers. In fact, the word *cyberbullying* has entered the lexicon of terminology in the bullying context. When schools have attempted to discipline students for inappropriate or offensive out-of-school Internet communications, students and their parents have challenged the school's power to regulate that expression. The good news for school districts is that courts are applying the familiar standards enunciated in *Tinker*, *Fraser*, and *Hazelwood* to students' cyberbullying. If districts know and apply the rules that courts have established for dealing with actual, face-to-face student expression, they will be safe in applying the same rules to virtual student expression (see Conn, 2002).

Conduct Not Protected by the First Amendment

Of course, bullies often do not stop at verbal aggression. Bullying frequently involves physical brutality. Bullies use size and physical superiority to intimidate and control. The First Amendment's guarantee of freedom of expression never extends to immunity for the physical conduct of bullies. However, bullies often do engage in physical aggression with impunity because their victims are too frightened to report the aggressive acts. Physical conduct, however, often begins with verbal aggression: when the words prove effective, acts follow.

The First Amendment does not protect bullies' physical acts, and administrators and teachers should not be misled to think it protects their vulgar, lewd, intimidating, or defamatory words, either. The verbal aggression of bullies that interferes with other students' ability to take advantage of educational opportunities falls outside the protection of the First Amendment, whether inside school or outside. Knowing the facts about what speech and expression the First Amendment does and does not protect is critical for educators.

Litigation Involving Bullying

Bullying itself is not against the law, unless states have adopted specific antibullying laws. Schools typically deal with bullying that crosses the line into behaviors prohibited by student codes of conduct or school district discipline policies.

Court decisions involving bullying are so far not numerous, but litigation, especially applying or challenging new state antibullying laws, may increase in the future. A Michigan court in September 2003 ruled that a state statute requiring school districts to adopt zero tolerance policies for students who engage in "verbal assaults" and a school district policy enacted in accordance with that law were both unconstitutionally overbroad and void because of their vague description of the behaviors proscribed.

The Michigan decision resulted when the parents of Alexander Smith, a junior at Mount Pleasant High School in eastern Michigan, filed suit alleging that his suspension for reading a commentary critical of the school's tardiness policy unconstitutionally abridged their son's First Amendment right to freedom of speech. Smith's parents also sought to have the school district's discipline policy declared unconstitutional.

Alexander got into trouble at lunchtime one school day in October 2000, after he read aloud at his cafeteria table his commentary on the school's tardiness policy. The policy, he had written, was made by "a Nazi" and supported by "teacher gestapos" engaged in "turd licking." He also discussed the principal's divorcing her husband and having an affair with another principal, calling her a "skank" and a "tramp." Other students outside his circle of supporters became upset and notified school officials.

The principal charged Alexander with "verbal assault" under the school's student code of conduct and suspended him for 10 days. The suspension was subsequently reduced to eight days, with the proviso that Alexander agree to examination and evaluation by a psychologist. The psychologist reported that Alexander had meant no harm and that the student did not have any pathology or psychological disorder. Alexander served his suspension and graduated in June 2002.

His parents initiated a lawsuit on his behalf after his graduation. They alleged violation of Alexander's constitutional rights and a declaration of the unconstitutionality of the school policy. The U.S. District Court for the Eastern District of Michigan agreed with Alexander's parents that the district policy on "verbal assaults" was unconstitutional, and it went a step further, declaring that the

Michigan statute on which the district's policy was based was also unconstitutional. Both the statute and the district policy, the court stated, were overbroad because they could be interpreted to prohibit constitutionally protected speech—for example, by curtailing speech, that questions the wisdom of school administrators or policies. Reviewing the holdings in the seminal student speech cases of *Tinker*, *Fraser*, and *Kuhlmeier*, the court found it "laudable" that the district sought to address confrontational, disruptive, and bullying speech, but reminded school officials that statutes and school policies that seek to regulate speech based on their disagreement with the views expressed violate the tenets of the First Amendment.

The court did read *Tinker*, *Fraser*, and *Kuhlmeier*, however, as providing the authority under which the school, independently of its "verbal assault" policy, could and should discipline Alexander. Speech that is lewd and profane, as were Alexander's comments about the principal's marital infidelity and insulting names directed at her, is subject to regulation by school authorities. The court noted that other students had been upset by Alexander's commentary and that even his reading the comment in the lunchroom could count as school disruption subject to proper disciplinary action under *Tinker*.

Given the difficulty of crafting state statutes that are simultaneously expansive enough to proscribe bullying speech in schools but do not unconstitutionally infringe on speech protected by the First Amendment, litigation over state antibullying statutes is bound to increase. State lawmakers and school officials charged with crafting policies must carefully review decisions such as *Smith v. Mount Pleasant Public Schools* and similar rulings on student speech issues in order to identify constitutionally acceptable language. In law, as in school bullying, words do count.

Annotated References and Resources

Constitutional and Statutory References

• The First Amendment to the U.S. Constitution provides that "Congress shall make no law respecting the establishment of religion, or prohibiting the free exercise thereof; or abridging the freedom of speech, or of the press; or the right of the people peaceably to assemble, and to petition the Government for a redress of grievances."

• The Fourteenth Amendment, Section 1, contains the due process and equal protection clauses, providing that "All persons born or naturalized in the United States, and subject to the jurisdiction thereof, are citizens of the United States and of the State wherein they reside. No State shall make or enforce any law which shall abridge the privileges or immunities of citizens of the United States; nor shall any State deprive any person of life, liberty, or property, without due process of law; nor deny to any person within its jurisdiction the equal protection of the laws."

• The Child Pornography Prevention Act (CPPA) of 1996 is 18 U.S.C. § 2252A, § 2256 (8) (B) and (D) (Supp. IV 1998). The original version of the act expanded the federal prohibition on child pornography to include not only pornography involving real children, but also any visual depictions, such as photos, films, videos, computer images or animations, that appeared to be minors engaging in sexually explicit acts. The Court specifically mentioned several Hollywood movies in which filmmakers arranged scenes or used youthful looking actors to suggest that children had engaged in sexual acts. The portions of the act relating to virtual child pornography were struck down as unconstitutional by the Supreme Court in *Ashcroft v. Free Speech Coalition*, 122 S. Ct. 1389 (2002). The Court reaffirmed that pornography produced with the involvement of real children can be criminalized, but that *virtual* child pornography "is not intrinsically related to the sexual abuse of children." Although many psychologists may disagree, the Supreme Court's ruling is controlling authority for all legal jurisdictions in the United States.

Court Decisions

• The Supreme Court enunciated the three prongs of the "*Miller* test" that legally define obscenity in *Miller v. California,* 413 U.S. 15 (1973).

• The Supreme Court decision that struck down a law prohibiting the sale of sexually explicit material to adults merely because it would be obscene for children, thereby upholding the right of adult access to pornographic materials, is *Ginsberg v. New York,* 390 U.S. 629 (1968).

• The Supreme Court discussed the "fighting words" doctrine in *Chaplinsky v. New Hampshire,* 315 U.S. 568 (1942).

• The Supreme Court defined "clear and present danger" in its decisions in *Brandenberg v. Ohio,* 395 U.S. 444 (1969) and in *Schenck v. United States,* 249 U.S. 47 (1919). A Michigan court applied the clear and present danger analysis to decide that the First Amendment did not protect student computer hacker Justin Boucher from imposition of school discipline. *Boucher v. School Board of the School District of Greenfield,* 134 F.3d 821 (7th Cir. 1998).

• The legal parameters of defamation were set out in the Supreme Court's decision in *New York Times Company v. Sullivan,* 376 U.S. 254 (1964).

• The three seminal student speech cases, decided by the U.S. Supreme Court in 1969–1988, are

– *Tinker v. Des Moines Independent School District,* 393 U.S. 503 (1969),

– *Bethel School District No. 403 v. Fraser,* 478 U.S. 675 (1986), and
– *Hazelwood School District v. Kuhlmeier,* 484 U.S. 260 (1988).

• Alexander Smith's case is *Smith v. Mount Pleasant Public School District,* 285 F. Supp.2d 987 (E.D. Mich. 2003). Other decisions involving acceptable student speech policies:

– *Killion v. Franklin Regional School District,* 136 F. Supp.2d 446 (W.D. Pa. 2001), where the court reminded the school district that students are entitled to due process—that is, notice and an opportunity to be heard—before being disciplined, and that the school must show that a student's expression caused material and substantial disruption of school operation before prohibiting that expression.

– *Saxe v. State College Area School District,* 240 F.3d 200 (3d Cir. 2001), where the court reaffirmed that schools cannot legally prohibit students from speaking out against the personal values of others. At issue were students' rights to criticize the gender orientation choices of other students. The court noted that schools can prohibit discrimination based on race, religion, national origin, gender, or age, as well as workplace harassment; but that schools cannot prohibit the expression of ideas simply because they are offensive or unpleasant.

– *Sypniewski v. Warren Hills Regional Board of Education,* 307 F.3d 243 (3d Cir. 2002), where the court reminded schools that they cannot prohibit student expression merely because of undifferentiated fears of disruption.

– *Coy v. Board of Education of the North Canton City Schools,* 205 F. Supp.2d 791 (N.D. Ohio 2002), where the court found that the school district's Acceptable Use Policy for school technology resources was unconstitutionally vague and overbroad because in using undefined words like "inappropriate," "belligerent," and "disrespectful," the policy did not give students adequate notice of what speech was prohibited, nor of the consequences for its use.

– *Schmader v. Warren County School District,* 808 A.2d 596 (Commwlth Ct. Pa. 2002), where the court affirmed the right of the school district to enforce its policy requiring students to report student misconduct that has the immediate potential of harm to the school community. The Schmader case is discussed more fully in Chapter 8.

– *Flaherty v. Keystone Oaks School District,* 247 F. Supp.2d 698 (W.D. Pa. 2003), where the court ruled that the school district wrongfully removed the student from his volleyball team for criticizing the opposing team in a chat room conversation that caused no material disruption in school operations. The district had to pay the student and his parents $60,000.00 in damages.

Journal Articles, Texts, and Commentaries

• Two clinical perspectives on recognition and treatment of bullying in the medical context are the following:

– Scott, J. U., Hague-Armstrong, K., Downes, K. L. (2003, April). Teasing and bullying: What can pediatricians do? *Contemporary Pediatrics, 20*(4), 105. Also available at www.contemporarypediatrics.com

– Jellinek, M. S. (2003, June). Treating both bullies and the bullied. *Pediatric News, 37*(6), 10. Also available at www.epediatricnews.com

• For a discussion of disciplining students for off-campus misbehavior, see Walsh, M. (2003, May 28). Misbehavior off campus raises issues. *Education Week, 22*(38), 1.

• For a discussion of student speech issues and the Internet, see Conn, K. (2002). *The Internet and the law: What educators need to know*. Alexandria, VA: Association for Supervision and Curriculum Development.

CHAPTER THREE

Sexual or Gender-Based Harassment of Students

More than 10 years ago, the American Association of University Women (AAUW) conducted its now famous study of sexual harassment in U.S. public schools: *Hostile Hallways: The AAUW Survey on Sexual Harassment in America's Schools* (1993). The study reported responses from a random sample of 1,632 boys and girls in grades 8–11 from 79 schools, which indicated that a pervasive culture of sexual harassment characterized U.S. secondary schools. Over 80 percent of females and over 70 percent of males responded that they had experienced some form of sexual harassment in school; more than one of every four students indicated that they had experienced sexual harassment "often."

Although criticized for including behaviors such as rumors, sexual comments, jokes or "looks," graffiti, and even questions about sexual identity among the descriptors of sexual harassment, the basic conclusions of the AAUW study have not been seriously questioned. In fact, subsequent studies have confirmed its overall findings. In a similar study conducted in Connecticut and released in 1995, even higher percentages of female students and about the same percentages of males reported having experienced sexual harassment in their schools. An update of the AAUW study in 2001 reported that four out of every five students in a nationwide survey of 2,064 students in nearly 100 schools had experienced either verbal or active sexual harassment in their schools, often under the noses of their teachers (Harris Interactive, 2001). Clearly, sexual harassment in schools is a problem.

Litigation is often viewed as a mechanism for remedying sexual harassment. Courts, however, will step in to recognize and deal with any kind of harassment only when the alleged harassment consists of conduct that either violates an individual's constitutional rights or is expressly prohibited by statutes applicable in the school context. Fortunately, both state and federal courts have decided a number of significant cases that now serve as precedents for individuals asserting school-related harassment that violates constitutional rights or statutes.

Federal Antiharassment Statutes

At the federal level, three laws specifically prohibit harassment in the school setting: Titles VII, IX, and VI. Although Titles VII and IX deal with harassment based on gender, while Title VI prohibits discrimination based on race, religion, or national origin, the legislative histories and purposes of all three are so interrelated that court rulings in lawsuits dealing with a violation of one often reference one or both of the others.

Titles VI and VII are part of the Civil Rights Act of 1964. Title VI provides protection against discrimination based on race, religion, or ethnic background in programs or activities receiving federal financial assistance. Although recent court decisions suggest that individuals can bring suit under Title VI only for intentional discrimination, complaints that an educational program or activity has a discriminatory effect, even if unintentional, can be made to the Office for Civil Rights, which investigates and reports violations to the Department of Justice. Title VII prohibits gender-based discrimination in the workplace. Teachers and other paid school district employees may bring suit under Title VII if they suffer adverse employment actions because of their race, color, religion, sex, or national origin. Because Title VII also applies in the workplace outside schools, receipt of federal funding is not a necessary precondition for Title VII to apply.

Often recognized as modeled on Title VI, Title IX, part of the Education Amendments of 1972, prohibits discrimination based on sex in educational programs or activities receiving federal funds. Although Title IX is most familiar to the public in the context of parity of school athletic programs for men and women, its stated purpose was to encourage women to participate in intellectually demanding programs of study on an equal footing with men. Individuals may bring an action in court if educational benefits or opportunities are denied on account of sex, or if gender-based harassment causes deprivation of educational opportunities or benefits.

Violation of Constitutional Rights

Many lawsuits alleging Title VI or Title IX violations are accompanied by Section 1983 causes of action, alleging that a school district or district employee or employees, acting "under color of state law" (i.e., in their collective or individual capacities as state actors), have deprived a student of his constitutional rights. Section 1983 states:

> Every person who, under color of any statute, ordinance, regulation, custom, or usage, of any State or Territory or the District of Columbia, subjects or causes to be subjected, any citizen of the United States or other person within the jurisdiction thereof to the deprivation of any rights, privileges, or immunities secured by the Constitution and laws, shall be

liable to the party injured in an action at law, suit in equity, or other proper proceeding for redress.

In other words, Section 1983 provides a remedy for violations of constitutional rights or rights under federal law. To state a claim that courts will recognize as a valid Section 1983 claim, a plaintiff must allege (1) that the conduct of a school district or a person acting under color of state law caused the violation, at least in part, and (2) that the conduct deprived the plaintiff of a right secured by the Constitution or a federal law of the United States. Proving a Section 1983 violation by a school district itself or by a school board acting as a local government entity is extremely difficult. Courts have ruled that school districts or school boards are guilty of Section 1983 violations only in the extreme cases in which they have established an official policy or tolerated a custom or practice that leads to, causes, or results in the deprivation of a constitutionally protected right. The "toleration" referred to by the courts, however, can be inaction in the face of repeated notification of problems. School district employees, such as principals and superintendents, are much more likely to be found liable under Section 1983 in their individual capacities as state actors than are school districts or school boards.

Other Causes of Action

State law claims can also accompany allegations of federal violations; for example, tort claims alleging negligence on the part of school officials or claims of negligent hiring directed against the district itself. Criminal charges are also possible in cases of harassment, especially sexual harassment.

The Rehabilitation Act (RA) and the Americans with Disabilities Act (ADA) deal with harassment of students or teachers in the school setting by virtue of age- or disability-related discrimination.

This chapter will discuss sexual or gender-based harassment of students in school or school-related settings. Harassment and discrimination of students and school employees based on other characteristics, including race, religion, sexual orientation, disability, and age, will be covered in subsequent chapters.

Title IX and Harassment

Although Title IX of the Education Amendments of 1972 is more familiar in the context of equality for female student athletes, it is also a powerful tool for redressing sexual harassment of students by either school personnel or peers. Patterned after Title VI, a federal statute prohibiting discrimination based on race, color, or national origin, Title IX gives private individuals the right to sue in court for redress of gender-based harassment by either opposite- or same-sex individuals.

Title IX provides that "[n]o person . . . shall on the basis of sex, be excluded from participation in, be denied the benefits of, or be subjected to discrimination under any educational program or activity receiving Federal financial assistance."

Courts have interpreted Title IX's "no person" language to apply also to employees; therefore, administrator-on-teacher, teacher-on-teacher, or student-on-teacher sexual or gender-based harassment may also be actionable under Title IX.

Proving a Title IX Claim

Although Title IX is expansive in its application, surmounting the burden of proof required under Title IX is difficult. Importantly, it is appropriations legislation. The legislative purpose of Title IX is to prevent discrimination in programs funded by federal funds. Title IX suits, therefore, must be brought against schools or school districts, not against individuals in their personal capacities. Courts are generally reluctant to impose liability on school districts, even where, for example, teacher-on-student harassment is egregious, for fear of subjecting districts to monetary damages that would deplete the public treasury and divert public funds disproportionately to a relatively few individuals. The strict rein on imposition of institutional liability for Title IX violations is easy to understand given the severity of the consequences for school districts that violate Title IX: federal funds are completely discontinued for any local education agency in violation of Title IX.

Title IX does not prevent students and parents or caregivers from suing responsible individuals based on other civil rights statutes or state tort laws (e.g., for a Section 1983 violation or for negligence or infliction of emotional distress); however, the courts will not hold school districts liable for its employees' actions merely because the school setting provided the opportunity or agency for the harassment. Authorities can also independently file criminal charges against either students or school district personnel for sexual harassment, sexual assault, or other sexual offenses.

Teacher-on-Student Sexual Harassment

When a student suffers harassment so severe that the school setting becomes an intolerable environment, parents and caregivers very naturally seek to bring the full force of the law against anyone and everyone involved, including the offending party or parties, other school employees, school administrators, and the school district itself. In cases of teacher-on-student sexual harassment, students or parents or caregivers acting on their behalf often sue for monetary damages, not only from the offending teacher but also from the principal, other school administrators, and the deeper pockets of the school district. Whether a court will hold the school district responsible under Title IX for sexual harassment by an employee depends on two critical factors: (1) the knowledge or information the district had regarding the alleged teacher-on-student harassment, and (2) how the district responded to that information.

The *Gebser* Decision

The court decision that firmly established these two prongs of school district liability under Title IX was handed down in 1998, almost seven years after teenager Alida Star Gebser of Lago Vista Independent School District in Texas was sexually abused by her high school English teacher. The teacher, Frank Waldrop, initiated sexual contact with Alida at her home, where he visited, ostensibly to deliver a book. Although the sexual relationship continued for over a year, Gebser did not report Waldrop's improper conduct to school authorities because, as she later testified, she was uncertain how to react. Besides, she added, she wanted to continue having him as a teacher.

Other parents complained to Waldrop's principal about sexually suggestive comments that Waldrop allegedly had made in class to other students. The principal advised Waldrop to be careful but did not report him to the district's Title IX coordinator. Not until several months later, after a police officer discovered Waldrop and Gebser having intercourse in a parked car and arrested Waldrop, did the district terminate Waldrop's employment. The Texas Education Agency then revoked his teaching license. During the whole time of Waldrop's relationship with Alida, the Lago Vista district had no antiharassment policy in place and no official grievance procedure for reporting sexual abuse.

When Alida and her mother finally filed suit against Waldrop and the school district in 1993, the U.S. District Court for the Western District of Texas rejected their Title IX claim against the district, reasoning that Title IX was enacted to counter systemic policies of discrimination, not the actions of one individual teacher.

In addition, the district court stated, the district had no knowledge of Waldrop's inappropriate relationship with Gebser. Alida and her mother appealed the decision.

Five years passed before the U.S. Supreme Court in 1998 ended the Gebsers' odyssey through the judicial system. The Court, while upholding the right of Alida and her mother to sue Frank Waldrop as an individual, refused to hold the school district liable on a theory of employer responsibility for its employees' actions or even because the district had a duty to know what was going on in its schools. Title IX was designed to prevent recipients of federal funds from using the funding in a discriminatory manner, the Court said, not to punish the independent misconduct of a teacher. School districts, according to the Court, are not liable for a teacher's sexual harassment of a student unless (1) an official of the district with authority to initiate corrective measures to address the discrimination has actual (i.e., concrete and specific) knowledge of the problem, and (2) that person makes an official decision to ignore the problem. These two elements—actual notice and deliberate indifference—are essential, the Court said, before a school district will be held liable for the sexual harassment of a student by its employee.

The majority opinion of the Supreme Court attributed only slight importance to the fact that Lago Vista had no formal antiharassment policy or official procedure for reporting abuse, stating that failure to adopt a policy did not constitute discrimination under Title IX. The Court suggested that administrative action by education agencies may have been in order, but without proof of actual notice and deliberate indifference by the district, the district would not be held liable for a Title IX violation.

Four justices of the Court strongly dissented in the *Gebser* decision, stating their fears that the outcome of the case would encourage school boards to insulate themselves from knowledge about sexual abuse in their schools. The dissenters expressed their view that Waldrop's relationship with Alida grew out of his role as an employee of the district and the authority that the district had delegated to him, and, therefore, the district was responsible for his conduct. They said the decision set "an exceedingly high standard" that future plaintiffs would have to meet to prevail against a school district in a Title IX lawsuit. This standard, coupled with uncertainty about the identity of the school official who must receive notice of the harassment, has stymied many potential plaintiffs.

Post-*Gebser* Decisions

Lower court decisions since *Gebser* have resolved some of the possible ambiguities in the *Gebser* language. Actual notice, the U.S. District Court for the District of Maine said, "requires more than a simple report of inappropriate conduct by a teacher." Who in the school district, for example, needs to receive actual notice of the sexual harassment? Who is "an official of the district with authority to initiate corrective measures"? Some plaintiffs in sexual harassment lawsuits have argued that they had complained about the harassment to other teachers or to the principal, and that the teacher or the principal was an official of the district who should have acted on their information. Districts have argued that neither teachers nor administrators could effect policy and that the school board itself needed actual notice.

Officials with Power to Correct

Several courts have ruled that principals are school officials with the power to initiate corrective measures to thwart teacher-on-student sexual harassment but that ordinary classroom teachers are not. However, in certain circumstances, teachers may become school officials with the requisite power. In a January 2000 ruling, the U.S. District Court for the Eastern District of Pennsylvania not only affirmed that a principal is the requisite school official to take corrective action but suggested that, when elementary school principal Geraldina Sepulveda hurriedly walked out of her office and directed a complaining parent to talk to the school's guidance counselor, the principal thereby delegated her authority to the counselor, who then may have become the *Gebser*-required school official.

The key issue seems to be that a principal has supervisory authority over teachers, with concomitant authority to question teachers about alleged inappropriate contacts with students. Other school administrators, such as curriculum supervisors or Title IX coordinators, may also exercise the requisite supervisory authority and, therefore, potentially satisfy the *Gebser* standard as an official of the district with authority to initiate corrective measures.

Deliberate Indifference

Another question that emerged after the *Gebser* ruling is what constitutes a school district's "deliberate indifference" to teacher-on-student sexual harassment? Does the action taken by a school official in response to information about the sexual harassment have to prevent future harassment? In other words, does school district response to notice of harassment have to be effective? What is a sufficient school district response to teacher-on-student sexual harassment, according to the courts?

In a Nebraska case of teacher-on-student harassment, the U.S. Court of Appeals for the Eighth Circuit ruled that the Omaha Public School District was not liable under Title IX for the actions of its high school teacher who had engaged in sexual relations with her female student because the district had not responded with deliberate indifference. The student, Janet Kinman, attempted suicide the summer after her sophomore year at Bryan High School in Omaha. She told her mother that one reason was that her teacher, Sheryl McDougall, was trying to convince her that she was gay. However, Janet and McDougall continued to associate after the

suicide attempt and began a sexual relationship. When the principal heard allegations of the affair, he removed Janet from
McDougall's study hall, temporarily ending the sexual relationship.
After Janet's graduation from high school, however, the relationship
resumed. The district was notified, although the court does not
specify how, and district officials investigated. They dismissed
McDougall for violating district policy prohibiting teachers from
engaging in sexual relations with former students within two years
of graduation, and the state of Omaha revoked her teaching license.

The district's actions in removing McDougall from the student's
study hall and in firing the teacher a year after her victim had graduated were sufficient to avoid liability, the court ruled, even though
they were ineffective and Janet's sexual abuse continued over the
course of several years. The court, however, allowed the victimized
student to pursue a Section 1983 civil rights claim against the former teacher in her individual capacity. The district, though, was off
the hook.

In a July 2000 decision, the Fifth Circuit Court of Appeals
refused to impose liability on the Dallas Independent School
District after one of its male teachers sexually molested several 3rd
grade boys. The court ruled that the principal had actual notice
dating back to at least 1986 that the teacher, John Earl McGrew,
may have inappropriately fondled several young boys. At that time,
the principal called a meeting with one of the alleged victims and
McGrew, but the teacher denied the allegation. Nevertheless, the
principal warned McGrew that if he repeated the behavior, he
"would be dealt with." The principal also checked with the student's classroom teacher, who reported that the student had not
alerted her to any misconduct by McGrew.

The principal took no further action against McGrew. Facts
subsequently came to light that McGrew had sexually molested
numerous male students between 1983 and 1987. He was

convicted in state court on one count of aggravated sexual assault and two counts of indecency with a child, and he was sentenced to one life sentence and two 10-year sentences. When victims and their parents brought a Title IX suit for damages against the school district, the court concluded that the principal was not deliberately indifferent, and, therefore, the district was not liable. The principal was wrong in believing McGrew's denial of involvement with the students, and her error "had tragic consequences," the court said, but the principal's ineffective response was not deliberate indifference. In fact, continued the court, many good faith but ineffective responses by administrators may serve to avoid district liability, including warning the teacher, notifying the student's parent, or removing the student from the teacher's classroom.

The Dallas Independent School District case demonstrates how unwilling courts are to second-guess and micromanage school districts. In hindsight, many educators would probably agree that calling a student into the principal's office to face his adult abuser would not be the best way to reach the truth of allegations of sexual misconduct. Yet the Court of Appeals for the Fifth Circuit found this a sufficient school district response to alleged sexual harassment of a student by his teacher.

What exactly does it take for a court to impose liability on a school district for teacher-on-student sexual harassment? Another case decided in 2000 was so egregious that avoiding liability was highly unlikely.

The U.S. District Court of the Northern District of Ohio ruled in January 2000 that the Akron City Board of Education violated not only Title IX by adopting a policy of deliberate indifference to teacher William Bennett's sexual harassment and abuse of students but also Section 1983, depriving the victims of their constitutional rights by tolerating a custom or condition that led to the students' abuse.

The court noted that the district's involvement began when the Akron Board of Education hired Bennett as a substitute teacher in 1985. Failing to do a background check, the district was unaware that Bennett's former superintendent in Collinsville, Virginia, had removed Bennett from contact with children after allegations that Bennett had taken a young male student to an isolated area for nearly an hour and subsequently stalked the boy.

After serving as a substitute teacher for several months, Bennett quickly obtained a full-time teaching position in the Akron schools. Almost immediately after his hiring, parents began complaining about his inappropriate contacts with young boys in his school. Even after frank and specific conversations with Bennett's former employers, the Akron Board of Education did not remove him from contact with students. In 1996, while a guidance counselor at an Akron high school, Bennett engaged in a lengthy homosexual relationship with a student. When the student, to conceal his homosexuality, denied the relationship, the board let the matter drop. Bennett subsequently continued his sexual predatory behavior for three more years, despite his principal's repeated entreaties to the board to remove Bennett from his school.

Although it seems almost unbelievable that a board of education would shut its eyes to such clear indications of sexual harassment of students as in Bennett's case *for 13 years*, the court at least was willing to allow suit to proceed against the district under both the statutory analysis of Title IX and the Section 1983 constitutional analysis, finding that the board's inaction directly caused the deprivation of the victims' constitutional rights. In a separate criminal suit, Bennett ultimately pleaded guilty to five counts of sexual battery and four counts of telephone harassment, and he was sentenced to jail.

School boards do have actual responsibility to take action under Title IX, against teachers and also against administrators who may be abusing children. Their responsibilities include promulgating effective policy guidelines for reporting possible sexual abuse of students and also for training school personnel in their use. The Supreme Court of New Jersey in July 2003 found the Elmwood Park Board of Education negligent in not taking action against Samuel Bracigliano, the principal of Gilbert Avenue Elementary School, who had covered his office door window to take photographs of male students in sexually suggestive poses. Bracigliano's suggestive and alarming sexual behaviors toward students had been matters of concern to staff members for years, although staff members, unaware of mechanisms in place for reporting his conduct, failed to do so. The plaintiffs' public administration expert witness faulted the superintendent for making "superficial" evaluations of Bracigliano and faulted the board for its failure to make frequent visits to the elementary school to evaluate staff performance and facilitate communication. The court found that the school board had failed to fulfill its most basic obligation: to protect the children in its care.

Student-on-Student Harassment

The judicially imposed burden of proving peer-on-peer sexual harassment is even more stringent than in teacher-on-student harassment situations. For many years, courts did not even recognize that districts could be liable under Title IX for peer-on-peer sexual harassment. The Supreme Court decision that finally declared that they could, and that defined the circumstances under which they would be liable, was *Davis v. Monroe County Board of Education*, a decision handed down one year after the *Gebser* decision.

The plaintiff in *Davis* was the mother of a 5th grade student, LaShonda Davis, who had suffered a prolonged pattern of gender-based harassment at the hands of a male classmate in her Georgia elementary school. The boy, identified by the court as G.F., made repeated attempts to touch LaShonda's breasts and genitals, at the same time making vulgar remarks about having sex with LaShonda. G.F.'s harassing behavior persisted for several months.

Both LaShonda and her mother reported each of the incidents to LaShonda's classroom teacher, who reassured mother and daughter that she had reported the inappropriate behavior to the principal. Nevertheless, no disciplinary action was taken against G.F. One day in physical education class, G.F. put a doorstop in his pants and acted in a sexually suggestive manner toward LaShonda. G.F. repeated his sexual innuendos in other classes, and his suggestive behavior escalated to his physically rubbing up against LaShonda in a sexually explicit way. LaShonda reported the incidents to several teachers, and her mother followed up with personal contacts to both the teachers and the principal. Again, no action was taken to reprimand or discipline G.F. or to separate him from contact with LaShonda. Other students also complained about G.F., but the principal continued to query LaShonda's mother as to why LaShonda was "the only one complaining."

LaShonda's ordeal finally ended when authorities charged G.F. with sexual battery, and the boy pleaded guilty to criminal sexual misconduct. LaShonda's grades had suffered a dramatic decline during her months of torment, and her father discovered a suicide note she had written as her reports of G.F.'s harassment were repeatedly ignored. When LaShonda's mother attempted to sue the school district for monetary damages under Title IX, the district court dismissed the suit, because it declined to recognize any circumstances under which a school district could be held responsible for student-on-student harassment. After multiple appeals, the Supreme Court finally acknowledged that school districts could indeed be held liable for discrimination caused by student-on-student harassment. However, the Court stated, the district could be held liable only for its own misconduct, not the misconduct of its students. The Court reaffirmed the actual knowledge/deliberate indifference standard established in *Gebser* and required that Davis prove that the district had remained idle in the face of known student-on-student harassment.

The fact that LaShonda's harasser was a fellow student, not a teacher, was significant. Underlying the *Gebser* ruling was the reasoning that for a district to be liable for sexual harassment, the harasser had to be someone over whom the school district had some authority or control. Moreover, the harassment had to have occurred in a context subject to the school district's control. G.F.'s conduct satisfied both these conditions, although not in the same way as a teacher's conduct. Because he was a student in the school, his behavior was subject to teacher authority, and the harassment occurred primarily during school classes.

A Third Element Required in Student-on-Student Harassment

In *Gebser*, the Supreme Court ruled that a school district could be held liable for teacher-on-student harassment only if an official with authority in the district had actual knowledge of the harassment and was deliberately indifferent to it. The *Davis* decision added yet another stipulation to insulate districts from liability. In cases of peer harassment, the Supreme Court ruled that the harassment must be "so severe, pervasive, and objectively offensive" that it undermines the victims' educational experience and effectively denies them equal access to the school district's resources and opportunities. Justice Sandra Day O'Connor, writing for the majority, noted that schools are not like the adult workplace. Schoolchildren, she stated, may "regularly" interact in a "dizzying array of immature . . . behaviors" that would not be acceptable among adults. Damages under Title IX, O'Connor continued, are not available for students' "simple acts" of teasing, shoving, pushing, insulting, and upsetting gender-specific conduct. However, the Court majority agreed that, in LaShonda's case, the harassment had risen to the judicially required level of severity. The school district, moreover, had effectively turned a blind eye to her suffering and to the suffering of other students as well.

Dissenting justices in *Davis* raised questions that are still somewhat unresolved today. In determining school district liability, how much "control" does the district have to be able to exert over the harasser? Public schools do not have a choice as to whom they accept as students, and districts do not have as much control over students as they do over their teachers and other staff. Courts seem to agree, however, that in student-on-student harassment, teachers have the requisite authority over students and that notification to teachers of alleged sexual harassment, even without involving the principal, is sufficient to put the district on notice of the problem.

How are schools to decide when harassment exceeds the bounds of normal immature interactions among students and reaches a severity that is actionable? Is sexual harassment pervasively severe only if a student's grades drop? Student-on-student harassment cases, even more so than teacher-on-student harassment lawsuits, are intensely fact dependent. The ages of the students involved as well as the actual facts are important. Nevertheless, juries, not school districts, are increasingly being called upon to decide such cases. As in teacher-on-student sexual harassment lawsuits, Section 1983 claims against school officials are often brought along with Title IX claims against the school district.

Post-*Davis* Cases

One of the first cases of student-on-student harassment decided based on the Supreme Court's decision in *Davis* was a lawsuit brought against School District Number 1 in Denver,

Colorado, by Penelope Murrell on behalf of her teenage daughter, Penelope Jones. The U.S. Court of Appeals for the Tenth Circuit had actually held the suit in abatement pending the ruling in LaShonda Davis's case.

Penelope Jones had physical disabilities, with spastic cerebral palsy and deafness in one ear. Intellectually and developmentally, the teenager functioned at the level of a 1st grader. Penelope transferred to George Washington High School after being sexually assaulted at her previous school. Her mother expressed concerns to school officials that her daughter would continue to be the victim of abuse, but they assured her that Penelope would be supervised and placed her in a special education class at George Washington.

Several months later, Murrell became alarmed when Penelope began receiving harassing telephone calls from a fellow special education student, "John Doe"; she notified school officials of her concerns. Teachers knew John Doe to be a significant disciplinary and behavioral problem, with aggressive sexual tendencies, and had been watching him because of his inappropriate conduct toward Penelope in class. Unfortunately, at about this time Doe was able to sexually assault the girl several times in school. On one occasion, a school janitor found them in the act in a secluded part of the school. Penelope, who was menstruating at the time, had bled and vomited during the assault. The janitor merely told them to clean up the mess and returned them to class. The teachers tied other clothing around Penelope's waist to cover her bloody clothes but never told her mother about the incident. At least one other assault occurred at the hands of Doe.

After Penelope had begun to engage in self-destructive behavior and entered a psychiatric hospital, her mother found out about the repeated assaults. Penelope eventually returned to school, and her mother met with the principal and Penelope's teachers, who were overtly hostile to her and refused to investigate her allegations.

The principal actually suspended Penelope for behavior that he said "was detrimental to the welfare, safety, or morale" of other pupils. Finally, Penelope's mother brought suit against the school district and school officials under Title IX and Section 1983.

Relying on the *Davis* decision, the Court of Appeals for the Tenth Circuit held that the principal and, through the principal, the district had actual knowledge of Penelope's harassment and were deliberately indifferent to it. Additionally, the court ruled that the harassment was sufficiently severe, pervasive, and objectively offensive to support a claim under Title IX. The Tenth Circuit declined to impose Section 1983 liability on the district, declining to recognize the teachers and principal as "policymakers" for the district, but allowed Penelope's mother to proceed on a Section 1983 claim against the teachers and principal in their individual capacities.

Circuit Judge Stephen Anderson appended to the majority opinion a prescient concurring opinion. Agreeing that the facts of this case were especially egregious and merited the court's opinion, Anderson cautioned that the "deliberate indifference" standard for plaintiffs was a "high hurdle" necessary because of "the myriad contacts . . . between teachers and students and between students and their peers" occasioned by school attendance. In other words, Anderson was pondering the problem of distinguishing Justice O'Connor's *upsetting gender-specific conduct* from true sexual harassment.

Court decisions since the *Murrell* and *Davis* rulings have continued to wrestle with distinguishing "normal" inappropriate gender-based conduct and peer sexual harassment that may be actionable under the law. Perhaps surprisingly, an alarming number of alleged Title IX violations arise from sexually suggestive behaviors between and among children in the elementary grades.

Marie O'Neill Manfredi, the mother of Frances O'Neill, certainly thought seven-year-old Frances was being subjected to unlawful sexual harassment in her elementary school in Mount

Vernon, New York. According to Manfredi, a 2nd grade male class-mate named Lamar engaged in "hitting, pushing and tormenting, verbally abusing, harassing, spitting, and sexually abusing" Frances. When the mother contacted the principal, he responded that she was not the first parent who had complained about Lamar and that Lamar was a "troubled kid." The court, however, took a different view, stating that the incidents recounted in Manfredi's testimony were "nothing more than the sort of mean-spirited teasing that troublesome little boys inflict from time to time on little girls who seem vulnerable." Six months after Manfredi's first complaints, the school finally transferred Frances to a different 2nd grade class. Frances finished the year successfully, and, the court noted, her attendance record improved.

"Jane Doe II" was not so fortunate as Frances. Jane's mother sued the Dallas Independent School District after a five-year-old male classmate sexually violated her five-year-old daughter by manually penetrating her vagina in physical education class, causing vaginal bleeding, hematuria, and pain. The school took no action against the boy; instead, the principal allegedly accused Jane of fabricating the story. Jane's mother removed her from the school after the same boy grabbed Jane a second time.

The school district argued that only one documented incident had actually occurred and that one instance of sexual harassment was insufficient to support a claim of Title IX liability. The court agreed that the *Davis* ruling meant that school districts would be held liable under Title IX only for deliberate indifference to sexual harassment that is "so severe, pervasive, and objectively offensive" that it deprives its victims of the educational opportunities or benefits of the school. However, the court ruled, forced manual vaginal penetration, even occurring only once, was "sufficiently severe."

The fact that harassed students are able to maintain classroom attendance and successfully participate in the educational program of the school with no perceptible decline of grades often enables a court to conclude that the alleged harassment was not sufficiently severe to trigger district liability under Title IX. Courts, however, will consider evidence of a student's drop in grades, clinical depression, or self-destructive or suicidal behavior as proving the severity or pervasiveness of sexual harassment.

Adequate Response in Student-on-Student Harassment

A Georgia court dealt with the issue not of whether the alleged inappropriate conduct rose to the level of sexual harassment, but of whether the school's response was adequate to avoid Title IX liability. Alexander Clark brought suit against the Bibb County Board of Education after the principal of Riley-Edison Elementary School "forgot" to notify him of several incidents in which a male classmate had inappropriately touched his 6th grade daughter's buttocks and upper body. The school took action after teachers had notified the principal of the problems but failed to advise the parents until some time afterward. The school's responsive action included conferencing with the boy and his mother, conducting class discussions on "personal space," and transferring the male student to another class. Clark was not satisfied. The court, however, stated that, although the school "could have taken more severe action," the court would not second-guess disciplinary decisions made by school officials unless those decisions were clearly unreasonable. Title IX, the court continued, does not confer on victims of student-on-student harassment the right to make specific remedial demands.

Harassment by Nonteaching School Personnel

When a Georgia school custodian sexually assaulted and raped a female middle school student, Lakisha Sherman, she and her mother brought suit in federal court asserting violations of Title IX and the Violence Against Women Act by the county, the school board, school officials, and the custodian. Lakisha's mother asserted that other parents had complained that the custodian had made improper sexual comments to their daughters and that those complaints should have alerted the district to the fact that Lakisha was in danger. Moreover, although security cameras monitored school corridors, the district had failed to install cameras at the storage shed where the assault occurred. The U.S. District Court in Georgia in January 2000 dismissed the Title IX claim against the district and all parties involved, stating that notice of the custodian's inappropriate conduct toward other students did not give the district actual notice that Lakisha would be a victim of assault. Moreover, the court refused to sustain a Section 1983 claim against the district because a district cannot be held responsible for the independent actions of its employees, even if, as in this case, the district did not perform a background check on the employee charged. The court allowed the suit to proceed against the custodian, in his personal capacity, under the Violence Against Women Act, but the school was not in any way liable under either Title IX or Section 1983.

The court's decision in Lakisha Sherman's case reinforces the courts' reluctance to hold school districts liable for their employees' actions, especially nonprofessional employees, unless they have specific notice of wrongdoing toward an identified individual. Even after receiving actual notice, a district can avoid liability by taking responsive action. Courts will accept a district's response so long as the action taken is not clearly unreasonable.

The Internet and Sexual Harassment

Patrick Carnes, a pioneer in the field of sex addiction, calls the Internet "the crack cocaine of sex addiction" (Hiltbrand, 2003, p. M1). Whether the courts will recognize Internet-enabled sexual harassment as a cause of action in Title IX lawsuits remains to be seen. However, sexually suggestive gossip and defamatory rumors are rife in Internet chat rooms frequented by K–12 students. Students' Internet "blogs" and e-mail also pose opportunities for cyberharassment. School districts must be vigilant in monitoring district-supported student access to Internet technology. Sexually harassing e-mails can also reach school mailboxes from remote senders, especially from "spammers" and "flamers." Courts have not yet directly addressed the legal responsibilities of school districts with respect to sexually harassing Internet communications written by students or directed toward students.

Annotated References and Resources

Constitutional and Statutory References

• Title VI of the Civil Rights Act of 1964, 42 U.S.C. § 2000 c, d, provides that "[n]o person in the United States shall, on the ground of race, color, or national origin, be excluded from participation in, be denied the benefits of, or be subjected to discrimination under any program or activity receiving Federal financial assistance." The court decision foreclosing private rights of action under Title VI, except in cases of intentional discrimination, is *Alexander v. Sandoval*, 121 S. Ct. 1511 (2001).

• Title VII of the Civil Rights Act of 1964, as amended, 42 U.S.C. § 2000 e – 2 (a) (1), prohibits discrimination "against any individual with respect to his compensation, terms, conditions, or privileges of employment, because of such individual's race, color, religion, sex, or national origin."

• Title IX of the Education Amendments of 1972, 20 U.S.C. § 1681, provides that "[n]o person . . . shall on the basis of sex, be excluded from participation in, be denied the benefits of, or be subjected to discrimination under any educational program or activity receiving Federal financial assistance." The court interpreted Title IX's "no person" language to apply also to employees in *North Haven Board of Education v. Bell*, 456 U.S. 512 (1982).

• The Civil Rights Restoration Act of 1988, 20 U.S.C.A. § 1687 provides that federal funds are completely discontinued for any local education agency (LEA) found to be in violation of Title IX.

• The Rehabilitation Act is 29 U.S.C. § 794. Section 504 of the Rehabilitation Act provides that students with disabilities receive educational support services.

• The Americans with Disabilities Act of 1990 (ADA), 42 U.S.C.A. § 12101, prohibits discrimination in employment against any "qualified individual with a disability." Coverage is not dependent upon an employer's receipt of federal funds.

• Section 1983, Title 42 U.S.C. § 1983 states that "Every person who, under color of any statute, ordinance, regulation, custom, or usage, of any State or Territory or the District of Columbia, subjects or causes to be subjected, any citizen of the United States or other person within the jurisdiction thereof to the deprivation of any rights, privileges, or immunities secured by the Constitution and laws, shall be liable to the party injured in an action at law, suit in equity, or other proper proceeding for redress . . . ." Section 1983 provides a remedy for violations of constitutional rights or rights under federal law, and plaintiffs may plead complaints of Section 1983 violations simultaneously with allegations of discrimination prohibited by federal statutes such as Titles VI, VII, or IX, the Rehabilitation Act, or the Americans with Disabilities Act.

Court Decisions

• Four decisions of the U.S. Supreme Court over the span of twenty-plus years define the Title IX legal rights of students sexually harassed in the school setting, either by teachers, school personnel, or other students:

1. *Cannon v. University of Chicago*, 441 U.S. 677 (1979), in which the Court ruled that Title IX is enforceable by means of lawsuits brought by private individuals; that is, that Congress intended to imply a private right of action under Title IX.

2. *Franklin v. Gwinnett County Public Schools*, 503 U.S. 60 (1992), where the Court stated that, under Title IX, a school district may be liable in damages for a teacher's sexual harassment of a student.

3. *Gebser v. Lago Vista Independent School District*, 524 U.S. 274 (1998), where the Court rejected theories of agency or vicarious liability as bases for institutional liability under Title IX, meaning that schools or school districts would not be responsible for the sexual harassment of students by its employees merely because the school employed the harasser. In order to hold a school or district liable for a teacher's sexual harassment of a student, the victim would have to show that the institution had actual notice of the harassment and was deliberately indifferent to it. The majority in *Gebser*, however, made clear that its holding did not limit the possible lawsuits an individual may bring against the school, the district, or the teacher under state law. Potential state law causes of action against the school or district can include negligence or negligent hiring; state law causes of action against the teacher may potentially include assault, battery, stalking, negligent infliction of emotional distress, and other civil and criminal charges.

4. *Davis v. Monroe County Board of Education*, 526 U.S. 629 (1999), where the Court extended the ruling in *Gebser* to apply to student-on-student harassment.

• In the years following the *Gebser* and *Davis* decisions, many state and federal courts weighed in with interpretations of the two Supreme Court decisions, fashioning rulings and remedies that comported with their reconciliation of the Supreme Court's pronouncements with the facts of the cases before them. Lower courts' reluctance to interfere in the decision-making processes of school districts, and their need to tolerate the egregious conduct of some school districts and school administrators for the sake of not depleting the public treasury with awards of monetary damages, made for some court rulings that make many educators uncomfortable. Following are the post-*Gebser,* post-*Davis* decisions referenced in the text of the chapter, in the order in which they are discussed:

– *Doe v. School Administrative District No. 19,* 66 F. Supp.2d 57 (D. Maine 1999), where the U.S. District Court for the District of Maine defined actual notice as requiring more than a report to a teacher.

– *Warren v. Reading School District,* 82 F. Supp.2d 395 (E.D. Pa. 2000). The January 2000 ruling of the U.S. District Court for the Eastern District of Pennsylvania affirmed the liability of the Reading School District based on the deliberate indifference of Geraldina Sepulveda, principal of the 10th and Green Elementary School, and let stand the jury's award of $400,000 in money damages against the district for the sexual harassment of a 4th grade student by his teacher Harold Brown. The court ruled that "supervisory conference" memoranda from both 1969 and 1995—noting the teacher's inappropriate contact with young male students and a parent complaint during the intervening years—put the principal on actual notice that Brown was engaging in sexually suggestive behavior with students; yet the district took no action. The teacher ultimately resigned when the 4th grader's mother discovered the teacher's inappropriate "play" behavior with her son, and reported the teacher to the county's Children and Youth Services.

– *Kinman v. Omaha Public School District,* 171 F.3d 607 (1999). In the decision, the U.S. Court of Appeals for the Eighth Circuit ruled that the fact that a teacher had actual notice as a wrong-doer is not pertinent to the requisite school district notice, where a female teacher convinced a female student she was gay, and had sexual relations with her. The court refused to impose liability on the school district, but allowed the student to pursue a Section 1983 action against the teacher as an individual, stating that coerced sex could rise to the level of a due process violation.

– *Doe v. Dallas Independent School District,* 220 F.3d 380 (5th Cir. 2000), which is the lawsuit against the Dallas Independent School District, alleging the district's deliberate indifference to the sexual abuse of several young male students by teacher John Earl McGrew. The plaintiffs sought further appeal to the U.S. Supreme Court, but the Court refused to hear the case in *Doe v. Dallas Independent School District,* 531 U.S. 1073 (2001). This kind of refusal by the Supreme Court is called a denial of *certiorari,* and signals that the Court does not disagree at this time with the lower court's conclusions of law.

– The Akron City Board of Education case is *Massey v. Akron City Board of Education,* 82 F. Supp.2d 735 (N.D. Ohio 2000). The court declined to award summary judgment to the school district on either Title IX or Section 1983 claims against it. The court also allowed state law claims of negligence, negligent hiring, and stalking against the district to proceed, refusing to grant sovereign immunity.

– The July 2003 decision of the Supreme Court of New Jersey is *Frugis v. Bracigliano,* 827 A.2d 1040 (N.J. 2003).

– Penelope Jones' case is *Murrell v. School District No. 1, Denver, Colorado,* 186 F.3d 1238 (10th Cir. 1999).

– Frances O'Neill's case is *Manfredi v. Mount Vernon Board of Education*, 94 F. Supp.2d 447 (S.D.N.Y. 2000). *Manfredi* cites *Bruneau v. South Kortright Central School District*, 163 F.3d 749 (2d Cir. 1998) for the proposition that the Second Circuit does not recognize Section 1983 actions brought in cases of peer-to-peer sexual harassment.

– Jane Doe II's case is *Jane Doe I v. Dallas Independent School District*, 2002 WL 1592694 (N.D. Tex.). Jane Doe I is the mother of Jane Doe II; the parent brought suit on behalf of her five-year-old daughter.

– Alexander Clark's case is *Clark v. Bibb County Board of Education*, 174 F. Supp.2d 1369 (M.D. Ga. 2001).

– Lakisha Sherman's case is *Sherman v. Helms*, 80 F. Supp.2d 1365 (M.D. Ga. 2000). The Violence Against Women Act is part of the Violent Crime Control and Law Enforcement Act of 1994, § 40302 (c), 42 U.S.C.A. § 13981 (c).

Journal Articles, Texts, and Commentaries

• The American Association of University Women Educational Foundation has to date funded two nationwide surveys to determine the prevalence of sexual harassment in U.S. secondary schools. Both surveys were conducted by Harris Interactive, an international market research, polling, and consulting firm, perhaps best known for their Harris Reports. The first survey is Harris Scholastic Research (1993). *Hostile hallways: The AAUW survey on sexual harassment in America's schools.* Washington, DC: American Association of University Women Educational Foundation. The second survey is Harris Interactive (2001). *Hostile hallways: Bullying, teasing, and sexual harassment.* Washington, DC: American Association of University Women Educational Foundation. Both reports are available for purchase at www.aauw.org/research/girls_education/hostile.cfm (accessed May 2004).

• The survey of sexual harassment in Connecticut secondary schools is Connecticut Permanent Commission on the Status of Women (1995). *In our own backyard: Sexual harassment in Connecticut's public high schools.* Hartford, CT: Author. The report is discussed on the Web site of the National Violence Against Women Prevention Research Center in "Sexual Harassment in Schools," an essay by Nan Stein, senior research scientist at the Center for Research on Women, Wellesley College, New York. The essay is posted at the Web site of the National Violence Against Women Prevention Research Center: www.vawprevention.org/research/sexharass.shtml (accessed May 2004).

• In discussing the Internet and sexual harassment, the availability of sexually explicit materials on the Internet and students' easy, potentially unsupervised access to them has become a matter of widespread discussion and debate. Patrick Carnes called the Internet "the crack cocaine of sex addiction" in an interview with David Hiltbrand. Hiltbrand, D. (2003, November 2) Online, out of control. *Philadelphia Inquirer*, p. M1.

CHAPTER FOUR

Other Forms of Harassment of Students

THE WORD "DISCRIMINATION" HAS TAKEN ON AN INTENSELY NEGATIVE connotation in our pluralistic society, but discrimination in the positive sense simply means discernment. A diner with a discriminating palate, a department store buyer with discriminating taste in fashion, a school assessment that discriminates between and among students' content knowledge: these phrases are unreservedly complimentary of the form of discrimination described. However, even in this favorable sense, the process of discrimination involves valuing some choices while devaluing or marginalizing others. Harassment of individuals, either by words or conduct, based on characteristics that the harasser scorns like race, color, national origin, sexual orientation, or religion, is the most extreme form of this devaluation. When such harassment effects discrimination in education, in the workplace, or in daily life, society cannot afford to tolerate it, much less compliment it. Both federal and state statutes now exist to prohibit harassment of students based on their race or ethnicity, gender orientation or sexual self-identity, or religious beliefs, and court decisions have further defined the reach of those statutes.

Harassment Based on Race or Ethnicity

Of all the sources of harassment, harassment based on race, color, or national origin may be the most insidious and damaging for students. The judiciary assumed an especially prominent role in attempting to stamp out discrimination in the public schools based on race in the landmark series of decisions in *Brown v. Board of Education* in the mid-1950s (Spital, 2003). However, some commentators contend that more recent court decisions have encouraged a trend toward increasing resegregation. The Harvard Civil Rights Project (2002) notes that public schools are less racially and ethnically diverse than they were 15 years ago. In almost every school district in the study, African American and Hispanic students have become more segregated from white students than they were only two decades ago.

Courts evaluate discrimination based on race, alienage, or national origin with exacting, or strict, scrutiny and tolerate such discrimination only for very serious, most compelling governmental interests. However, despite court decisions prohibiting such discrimination, race-based discrimination in schools persists. African Americans are not the only victims; Asian, Hispanic, Middle Eastern, and even Caucasian students have been victimized.

As in cases of gender-based or sexual harassment, individuals who are suffering racial harassment in schools may turn to the Office for Civil Rights (OCR) of the U.S. Department of Education (DOE) for help. The Fourteenth Amendment guarantees equal protection of the law, despite race, color, or national origin. Harassed individuals may also claim a Section 1983 violation of their civil rights by persons or entities acting under color of state law, or they may bring a cause of action under related sections of the Civil Rights Act of 1964. One of these sections is Title VI.

Title VI and Racial Discrimination

Like Title IX, Title VI is a federal statute that forbids discrimination by entities that receive federal funds. However, whereas Title IX prohibits discrimination based on a person's sex or gender, Title VI prohibits discrimination based on race, color, or national origin.

Part of the Civil Rights Act of 1964, Title VI provides that "[n]o person in the United States shall, on the ground of race, color, or national origin, be excluded from participation in, be denied the benefits of, or be subjected to discrimination under any program or activity receiving Federal financial assistance."

Because schools definitely qualify as programs or activities receiving federal financial assistance (although many educators would argue not enough), Title VI acts to protect students from race- or ethnicity-based discrimination that would interfere with their participation in school activities or diminish their opportunity to receive an education. Because the language of Title VI refers to "person[s]," Title VI also protects school personnel from racial or ethnic discrimination. Any person who is discriminated against on the basis of race, color, or national origin can bring a Title VI complaint to an administrative agency such as the Office for Civil Rights or to any state Department of Education. In those cases in which individuals believe the racial or ethnic discrimination was intentional, they may also bring a cause of action in the courts against the person or entity they believe is responsible.

Harassment based on race, color, or national origin can effect the discrimination referred to in Title VI. If a bully persistently taunts, defames, picks on, shoves, physically intimidates, or steals from Asian, Jewish, Hispanic, white, or black students, because of their race or ethnicity, the victims, or caregivers acting on their behalf, have the right to take legal action under Title VI. However, whether the court will decide that a school official or the federal funding recipient (i.e., the school district) has violated Title VI involves the same two-pronged analysis of whether the district received "actual notice" and whether it responded with "deliberate indifference" as required in Title IX cases.

Litigation Involving Racial Discrimination in Schools

The U.S. Court of Appeals for the Second Circuit succinctly set forth the requisite legal analysis in a 1999 racial harassment case in which parents alleged that the Wallingford, Connecticut, school district had demoted their son, a black 1st grade student, to kindergarten after only nine days in a new school solely because of race. Cook Hill Elementary School originally placed the student, Ray Gant Jr., in 1st grade after he moved to Cook Hill from Meriden, Connecticut, where he had been a 1st grade student. Neither the school district nor the Gants denied that the students at Cook Hill Elementary School were predominantly white—98–99 percent white, in fact—or that white students, and possibly even adults, subjected Ray Jr. to racial name-calling.

After school authorities failed to respond adequately to their allegations that their son was the victim of intentional racial discrimination, the Gants brought suit in federal district court, alleging denial of equal protection of the law and violations of their son's civil rights. The court granted summary judgment to the district, effectively stating that the Gants could not win their case under even the most favorable interpretation of the facts. Undeterred, the Gants appealed to the U.S. Court of Appeals for the Second Circuit.

Incorporating the Title IX and Title VII Standards

The Court of Appeals began its analysis by stating that for the Gants to succeed on a claim of race discrimination based on the school's responses to their son's race-based harassment in the school environment, they must show that the school was deliberately indifferent to the harassment, as in Title IX suits. The deliberate indifference standard would be met, the court stated, if the Gants could show that the school's response to the harassment was "clearly unreasonable in light of the known circumstances," echoing the "actual notice" requirement under Title IX analysis.

The Gants were upset over the school's responses to name-calling and racial epithets uttered by their son's peers in school, but they particularly noted what they felt was the principal's inadequate response to an incident that had occurred at a school bus stop, where a white parent commented that her child would "have to ride with a nigger." The principal testified that, other than checking with Ray Jr.'s teacher, she had taken no action because she felt that she had no authority over the parent's actions outside school. The court accepted this explanation.

More serious in the court's consideration was the demotion of Ray Jr. to a kindergarten class, despite the fact that he had attended 1st grade in his former school and was of the appropriate age for 1st grade. The court considered Ray Jr.'s demotion despite his age and former placement as *prima facie* evidence of racial discrimination. (*Prima facie* is Latin for "on the face of it." Courts use the phrase to signify a set of facts that appears at first glance to support the plaintiff's assertion.)

With this *prima facie* evidence analysis, the court incorporated not only the Title IX standards of actual notice and deliberate indifference, but also the "burden-shifting" analysis used in Title VII employment discrimination analyses, illustrating just how complex and convoluted analysis of discrimination cases can become.

Under a Title VII burden-shifting analysis, the plaintiff must first show that discrimination likely occurred (the *prima facie* requirement). The burden then shifts to the defendant to show a legitimate, nondiscriminatory reason for its actions. In other words, the court was asking the school district to show that race was not the reason Ray Jr. had been transferred to kindergarten.

The district met its burden of showing a legitimate, nondiscriminatory reason for Ray Jr.'s transfer to kindergarten by producing school records demonstrating that he had been several months behind the average 1st grader, especially in reading, and that his academic placement in 1st grade was causing him stress. The court found the record of Ray Jr.'s academic difficulties overwhelming; even after his transfer to kindergarten, Ray was still having academic problems. The transfer to kindergarten was academically, not racially, motivated, the majority found.

A dissenting judge, however, called attention to the "arguably unusual" transfer that the majority accepted as justified. Circuit Judge Sonia Sotomayer, herself a Hispanic, stated that she considered the treatment that "this lone black child" had received as "unprecedented and contrary to the school's established policies." Every other student in the elementary school who had been experiencing academic difficulties received transitional help, but after only nine days, the principal decided that Ray Jr.'s academic difficulties were beyond remedial help and put him back into a grade that he had already completed. Academic deficiency was a pretext, Sotomayer stated, for racial discrimination. The school did not give Ray Jr. a chance to succeed, she said.

Identifying Racial Harassment

Allegations of racial harassment are difficult to resolve. Courts must decide based on factual evidence. Sometimes the demeanor of witnesses is helpful, but at the appellate level, only the record is present. Are some teachers or school officials racially biased? Certainly. Do some teachers or school officials act out those biases? Yes. White students in a predominantly white school may harass students of color; students of color may also harass white students. Whatever the racial tenor, the pervasive problem of distinguishing "mere teasing" and "simple bullying" from intentional discriminatory harassment persists.

During his 2nd and 3rd grades at Kennelly Elementary School in Hartford, Connecticut, several black and Hispanic students persistently harassed Joshua Crispim, a white student, shutting doors in his face and pushing him around in school. The harassment continued outside school, too, with kids throwing him down on the grass, kicking him, and calling him names such as "cracker." His mother met with the principal at least 10 times about the assaults, but despite assurances that the students would be reprimanded, nothing happened. Finally, his mother removed Joshua from Kennelly, and the family moved to another school district. After the move, acting on her son's behalf, Joshua's mother sued the principal and two of his teachers, alleging violations of Joshua's civil rights and seeking to recover moving costs.

Examining Joshua's Section 1983 claim, the court introduced a new element into the analysis: Did the school have a "special relationship" with Joshua that imposed on school officials an affirmative duty to protect him? If not, did school authorities affirmatively act to create an opportunity for harm to Joshua that would not have existed otherwise (the "state-created danger" theory)? The "special relationship" referred to, according to prior U.S. Supreme Court decisions, would be that which a prisoner would have with his jailers or that which a foster child would have with the state as guardian. With *special relationship* defined in those terms, the court said that no such relationship had existed between Joshua and the school and that, moreover, the school had not taken any action to make Joshua any more vulnerable to harm than he already was. After all, school officials had punished Joshua's harassers by depriving them of playground recesses "once in a while." The court in August 2003 determined that the reported incidents of harassment were "nothing more than adolescent bullying." Joshua's case is a reminder that outdated beliefs about bullying and harassment as "normal" parts of school and growing up are still prevalent in the judiciary.

Different Treatment

When racial tensions in a school are high, fights between students are almost inevitable. However, when white and African American students clash openly, and the school suspends only the African American students, a charge of racial discrimination is inevitable.

Charles and Chase Bryant, African American brothers, brought suit against their Garvin County, Oklahoma, school district for their suspension under the school's fight policy, alleging intentional racial discrimination in violation of Title VI. The Tenth Circuit accepted the suspension of the African American students and not their white opponents as a *prima facie* case of racial discrimination. The situation, however, was even more complex than a onetime brawl. The brothers also alleged that the school administration had tolerated a hostile racial environment that deprived black students of full participation in the educational process.

The school's fight policy provided that students guilty of a second fighting offense in the course of a semester would be suspended for the remainder of the semester. Although suspending only the black students after the fight in question appeared to be racially motivated, the school met its burden of proving absence of intent to discriminate by showing that (1) the black students, and not the white students, involved in the fight had thereby committed their second fighting offense, and (2) of approximately 10 students involved in two or more fights per semester over the last 10 years, four were African American students (including the Bryants) and six were Caucasian. All were suspended. The court found that the school district had not violated Title VI by intentionally discriminating against the Bryants.

The issue of hostile educational environment remained at the fore. The Bryants alleged that the school allowed the presence of racial slurs, swastikas, and *KKK* initials carved in school furniture and on the lockers and notebooks of African American students. The school also allowed Caucasian males to wear T-shirts bearing the Confederate flag emblem, in violation of the school dress code prohibiting disruptive clothing, despite complaints by students and parents. The question for the court was, Did the school's inaction in these matters rise to intentional discrimination? If not, if the school's inaction concerning these matters was simply a facially neutral policy that had had a disparate impact on African American students, then Title VI afforded the Bryants no private remedy through the court system.

However, the court did not view the school's failure to deal with the overt racism expressed in the racial epithets and the Confederate flag T-shirts as the adoption of a facially neutral policy. The court ruled that students and parents had made the principal aware of the racial issues and that students, and possibly even teachers, had been acting in an intentionally discriminatory manner toward black students. The school's choice not to act may have incurred Title VI liability. "Choice implicates intent," the court stated. The court in July 2003 allowed a Title VI cause of action against the school to proceed, suggesting that the school's failure to deal with racist issues created a hostile environment for black students and may have constituted intentional racial discrimination.

Harassment Based on Sexual Orientation

Although sexual orientation is a sex-related issue, discrimination based on one's actual or perceived sexual orientation is legally different from gender-based or sexual harassment. Persons with a homosexual orientation do not constitute a legally definable, constitutionally protected class. Title IX does not explicitly protect individuals harassed because of sexual orientation. The Fourteenth Amendment, however, still serves to protect the rights of gays, lesbians, and bisexuals to be free from discriminatory harassment. Although courts will not apply intense scrutiny to proferred reasons for discrimination based on sexual orientation, the Supreme Court has upheld constitutional protection from discrimination based on actual or perceived sexual orientation.

In 1996, in one of the earliest court cases to take a school district to task for failing to protect a student from peer harassment based on gender orientation, the court admonished the district for responding to the homosexual student's complaints less earnestly than similarly situated nonhomosexual students. Jamie Nabozny was a 7th grader in the Ashland Public School District in Ashland, Wisconsin, when he realized he was gay. He was almost immediately subjected to both verbal and physical harassment at the hands of his fellow students. One day in science class two boys knocked him to the floor, held him down, and conducted a mock rape while 20 other students looked on and laughed. When he reported the mock rape to Principal Mary Podlesny, she told him "boys will be boys."

Nabozny repeatedly reported his harassment to his counselor and to other school officials, asking them to protect him and to punish his tormentors. Although on several occasions they promised to protect him, they did nothing. Evidence at trial even suggested that these same school officials mocked him. As the harassment continued into the 8th grade, Nabozny attempted suicide. After hospitalization, the young man returned to school at a private Catholic school, but it did not offer classes beyond grade 8. Nabozny had to finish his schooling at the Ashland public high school, where harassment of his sexual orientation continued. Finally, he filed a Section 1983 lawsuit in court, alleging that the school officials and the district had violated his rights under the Fourteenth Amendment to equal protection and due process.

Though the court declined to recognize Nabozny's due process claims, they allowed his suit to proceed under a theory of deprivation of equal protection because, the court said, the school district had treated male and female victims differently, and the district could show no rational basis for the different treatment. The district finally settled the lawsuit with Nabozny, paying him $900,000.

Four years later, a district's egregious lack of response to peer harassment of a student based on perceived gender orientation was detailed in a Minnesota district court. The student, Jesse Montgomery, recounted how fellow students and even school bus drivers had taunted him for nearly 11 years, causing him to stay home from school, avoid the school bathrooms and cafeteria, not play intramural sports, and forgo school-provided bus transportation.

Jesse sued the school district for failing to prevent his torment at the hands of his classmates who, beginning in kindergarten, had subjected him to severe and unrelenting verbal abuse that escalated to physical abuse by 6th grade. Peers called him "faggot," "queer," "femme boy," "fairy," and "pansy." They punched him, tripped him, superglued him to his seat, rubbed up against him, and grabbed his legs, inner thighs, buttocks, and crotch. When he and his parents reported the incidents, the school responded by issuing ineffective reprimands to the offending students or sending them to the office. At one point in middle school, the principal required Jesse to attend group discussions on responding to harassment, forcing him to miss his favorite academic classes. Finally, after Jesse filed a formal complaint against the district when he was in 10th grade, the school suspended one of the harassers for five days and another for one day. Jesse finally transferred to another school to finish high school, and he and his parents filed suit in court, alleging violations of both state antiharassment laws and Title IX.

The district argued that Title IX proscribes gender-based or sexual harassment and not gender orientation harassment, a technically correct reading of the statute. The Minnesota court had no difficulty finding that the district's insensitivity to Jesse's harassment constituted harassment discrimination under Minnesota law and in violation of the Fourteenth Amendment. The court also found that the school district had violated Title IX.

Affirming that Title IX protects students from peer-to-peer sexual harassment only, not actual or perceived gender orientation harassment, the court ruled that the kind of conduct Jesse was subjected to was discrimination "on the basis of sex," within the meaning of Title IX. Students engaged in harassing Jesse from kindergarten, the court noted, when children were highly unlikely to understand the difference between homosexuality and heterosexuality. More likely, the court said, peers had harassed Jesse because he exhibited feminine personality traits and did not fit their stereotypical notions of how a boy should behave. Later, when middle school boys grabbed his crotch and physically subjected him to simulations of anal rape, the harassing conduct rose to gender-based, not merely gender orientation, harassment. The court ruled that the "explicitly sexual acts directed at [Jesse] constitute[d] more than ordinary juvenile bullying" and were sufficiently severe to interfere with his education, despite his ability to maintain average grades. "[G]rades are not the sole benefit to be derived by a student from an educational experience," acknowledged the court.

The Gay-Straight Alliance Network, an organization whose goal is to eliminate homophobia and intolerance in schools, helped a homosexual California high school student mount a Section 1983 claim for punitive damages against his school superintendent for reckless disregard of the student's civil rights in tolerating and fostering a homophobic environment in the Visalia Unified School District. Gay students were spit upon, had objects thrown at them, and experienced death threats, all with the approval and sometimes participation of teachers. The district's official reaction to complaints was to encourage homosexual students to pursue independent studies in alternative settings.

The Visalia Unified School District paid $130,000 to student George Loomis to settle his lawsuit alleging that he had suffered a pattern of harassment from students and teachers and that school officials had failed to respond appropriately (Walsh, 2002). Staff members must undergo training on how to prevent sexual orientation harassment, and students must attend peer-mediated sessions on gender orientation harassment. When advocacy groups are permitted by the court to take up students' causes, as, for example, when the American Civil Liberties Union takes on student expression cases, the students' appearance in court increases the likelihood of a favorable outcome. This case in California proves the point.

Though gender orientation harassment is the topic, a reminder is in order that school districts cannot abridge the free expression rights of homosexual students. A U.S. district court in Nevada was the first to acknowledge that gay students may have a constitutional right to disclose their sexuality at school.

Derek Henkle, a student at Galena High School, appeared on a local access channel program called *Set Free* to discuss his experiences as a gay high school student. Antigay harassment at school began immediately after his television appearance. In one incident several students called him "fag," "butt pirate," and "fairy" and lassoed him around the neck and threatened to drag him behind a truck. When Henkle escaped and reported the incident to the assistant principal, the school official laughed. After other intimidating incidents, Henkle requested a transfer, which was granted on the condition that he "keep his sexuality to himself." This admonition was repeated at his new school, where his principal told Henkle to "stop acting like a fag." A second transfer failed to stop Henkle's harassment or the schools' orders to keep quiet about his gender orientation, despite school officials' actual witnessing several students physically attack Henkle. Finally, the district enrolled Henkle in an adult education program at a local community college, where he was unable to qualify for a high school diploma.

Henkle finally sued the district and school officials, alleging violations of equal protection guaranteed by the Fourteenth Amendment and violations of his First Amendment right to free speech. When the court ruled that Henkle had a legally cognizable cause of action for violation of his right to free speech, and a possibility of obtaining punitive damages, the district agreed to settle Henkle's lawsuit for $451,000 (Walsh, 2002).

In another case, an Arkansas teenager named Thomas McLaughlin recently settled a lawsuit against the Pulaski County Special School District, which disciplined him for speaking to his classmates about his sexual orientation. Fourteen-year-old Thomas will receive $25,000 (or his lawyers will receive $25,000), an apology from school officials, and a clearance of his disciplinary record (Trotter, 2003).

State Statutes and Special Schools

By January 2004 at least nine states had passed laws against discrimination or harassment in schools based on sexual orientation or gender identity. Many national advocacy groups—including the American Civil Liberties Union; the Anti-Defamation League; the Gay-Straight Alliance Network; the Gay, Lesbian, and Straight Education Network; Human Rights Watch; the Lambda Legal Defense Fund; and the Transgender Law Center—support lesbian, gay, bisexual, and transgender (LGBT) students' rights to be free of harassment in schools. Such groups report that sexual orientation harassment is a pervasive problem in schools. For example, Lambda Legal Defense Fund (2002), a national advocacy organization for individuals with nontraditional gender identity or orientation, reports that over 60 percent of LGBT students felt unsafe at school in a survey of 904 LGBT students from across the United States. The survey results also shed light on the basis of their fears: 83 percent reported experiencing verbal harassment at school because of their sexual orientation; 63 percent had been inappropriately touched or subjected to sexual comments; and 42 percent had been shoved or pushed in gender orientation-related confrontations, and half of those had been actually punched, kicked, or injured with a weapon. Many students reported that school administrators and teachers either ignored or even actually participated in the harassment. A more recent survey in 2003 reiterated the findings of the 2001 survey.

Data such as that led to the August 2003 opening of the first, fully accredited public high school for LGBT students: the Harvey Milk School in New York City. Originally established as a private alternative school by the Hetrick-Martin Institute, a private advocacy group for gay rights, Harvey Milk became a state-supported public school after the New York City Department of Education contributed $3.2 million in renovations. Harvey Milk is a small school—current enrollment is about 100 students—but it provides after-school programs for approximately 2,000 more LGBT students.

Although New York has jumped to the forefront in educating LGBT students, not all school districts embrace equal rights for LGBT students, and even when they do, district stakeholders may not agree. The Westminster School Board in Orange County, California, made national headlines in 2004 when it refused to add to its antiharassment policy a prohibition against discrimination based on "perceived gender characteristics," as mandated by California law. Facing a loss of $8 million in annual state and federal funding, the board finally capitulated (Zehr, 2004). Feelings in the community, however, still run strong.

Feelings in a central Pennsylvanian rural community culminated in a lawsuit to force the State College Area School District to revise its antiharassment policy by removing its prohibition against students criticizing homosexuality and homosexual students. Fundamentalist Christians in the community argued that the policy impermissibly prevented them from speaking out against homosexuality, which they believed it was their religious duty to do.

In an attempt to cultivate an atmosphere of mutual respect, the district's student speech policy had prohibited harassment "based on race, religion, color, national origin, gender, sexual orientation, disability, or other personal characteristics." Though the court upheld the right of the district to prohibit harassing speech based on race, religion, color, national origin, gender, and disability, citing Titles VI and IX and the Rehabilitation Act, it ruled that the policy is unconstitutionally overbroad where it prohibits disparaging speech based on personal *values*. The district may try to keep students from insulting one another based on personal physical characteristics, the court said. That may be futile or just plain "silly." However, a basic tenet of the Constitution's protection of freedom of speech means that schools cannot prohibit students from expressing opinions about morality.

Harassment Based on Religious Beliefs

While students who experience gender orientation discrimination in schools may be at a legal disadvantage because they lack definition as a constitutionally protected class, students who are harassed in school because of their religious beliefs may be at a greater legal disadvantage for a different reason: the First Amendment. The First Amendment prohibits public schools from favoring one religion over another. In addition, public schools may not become excessively entangled in religion or religious issues. What this has meant in at least one instance is that while a group of LGBT students may attend a special public school where they are free from gender orientation harassment, a very strict, recognizable religious group often harassed for their religious beliefs may not have their own state-supported school.

In 1989, recognizing the needs of the Satmar Hasidic Jews for a school to serve their group's special education students, the New York state legislature passed a law creating the Kiryas Joel Village School District, a school district whose geographic boundary encompassed the 320 acres owned and inhabited entirely by families of the Satmar Hasidim enclave. The Satmars are "vigorously religious" Jews who interpret the Torah strictly. They speak Yiddish, segregate the sexes outside the home, avoid television and radio, and dress in distinctive ways. Most Satmar children in the Kiryas Joel community attended private religious schools, but the private schools could not accommodate the Satmar children with disabilities. Enrolling the disabled Satmar children in public schools of the Monroe-Woodbury Central School District was unthinkable because of the "panic, fear, and trauma" the children experienced when separated from their unique community.

However, the separate public school district was not to be. Challenged in the courts as prohibited by the First Amendment, the district was dissolved. The Supreme Court ruled that establishment of New York's Kiryas Joel Village School District was not neutral with respect to religion and thereby violated the Establishment Clause of the First Amendment. Although the state legislature tried to revive the concept of the separate school district after the Supreme Court's decision, its subsequent efforts were also challenged on First Amendment grounds and failed to pass constitutional muster.

In keeping with the First Amendment's championed separation of church and state and its prohibition on state support of religion, students who allege school district liability for harassment because of religious beliefs may face a stiff uphill battle in the courts. In a recent case in the Western District of Pennsylvania, a middle school student, Nicole Lindsley, alleged that the Girard School District, along with its principal, assistant principal, and guidance counselor, had violated her constitutional rights and her rights under several federal statutes by failing to protect her from harassment based on her vigorously espoused Christianity. Nicole wore an unmistakably religious article of clothing to her 7th grade class nearly every day. Nicole's T-shirts exhorted her classmates to "Get a Life. Follow Jesus" or "Praise the Lord," among other refrains. Her peers harassed her verbally, calling her "Jesus freak" and "bitch"; threatened to stab her; doused her with cologne and threatened to light her on fire; and pelted her house with eggs. When Nicole complained in class about an assignment involving witches, her teacher told her that if she did not like the assignment, to go to another school. When Nicole's mother complained to the assistant principal, he told her that Nicole "was asking for trouble, wearing those shirts." By the end of the semester, Nicole was in emotional distress and failing almost all her academic subjects.

The Pennsylvania court, although recognizing that Titles IX and VI hold school districts responsible for preventing sexual or racially based harassment of students, declined to extend either federal statute to afford a remedy to Nicole, stating that schools need not accept responsibility for "private harms." The court noted that the district had not interfered with Nicole's First Amendment freedom to express her opinion by wearing her religious clothing and that Nicole had not ceased wearing the clothing because of alleged harassment. Nicole also brought claims under the Individuals with Disabilities Education Act (IDEA) and other disabilities rights statutes. The court dismissed those claims until she had exhausted available administrative remedies. This case demonstrates that claims of harassment based on religion are not likely to prove successful in the courts.

Harassment Based on Disability

If instead of alleging a religion-based claim of harassment Nicole had brought a claim of harassment based on an identified and documented disability, she may have received a more sympathetic hearing for her claim. IDEA, the Rehabilitation Act of 1973 (RA), and the Americans with Disabilities Act (ADA) are three powerful federal statutes in the service of plaintiffs with disabilities. However, IDEA, RA, and ADA may require exhaustion of administrative remedies before courts will entertain suits against school districts that fail to respond when notified that a child with disabilities is being bullied or harassed. The impetus for requiring administrative process is that courts feel that the administrative agencies, local school districts, hearing officers, and state educational agencies that routinely deal with the business of education have more educational expertise than do courts of law.

Exhaustion of administrative remedies is not required, however, under certain circumstances where it is improbable that appropriate relief can be obtained through administrative channels. For example, a New York court in 2002 allowed the parents of Arley McAdams to pursue a remedy in court without exhausting administrative procedures for relief because the applicable administrative body, the school district, had persistently failed to act with respect to their complaints that their son was being bullied and harassed by regular education classmates.

Arley was a 5th grader with learning disabilities at the Joseph A. Edgar Intermediate School. His Individualized Education Plan (IEP) provided that Arley would be "mainstreamed" in regular education classes while receiving resource room services for 40 minutes each day. Unfortunately, Arley fell prey to a group of student bullies who beat him up, inflicting bruises that he explained to his parents as the result of accidental falls. Although he did not tell his parents about the harassment, Arley did tell school officials.

From April 1997 to November 1998, bullies subjected Arley to increasingly escalating episodes of physical violence, ganging up on him in the school playground, kicking him and stepping on his hands, and eventually fracturing his neck, back, and kneecaps. The school district placed Arley in home instruction. When he recovered, the district recommended resuming his placement in regular education classes.

Arley's parents disagreed with the planned placement and instituted special education due process hearings under IDEA. In addition, they brought suit in federal court alleging that the school district was a hostile environment for Arley because the district had disregarded his fears, physical injuries, and harassment at the hands of his classmates.

The court allowed the parents' suit to proceed without exhausting administrative remedies under the "futility exception," because the school district had persistently refused to deal with the McAdamses' concerns, and two years had passed without a resolution of their issues. Whether courts can ever order recompense sufficient to recover two years of a child's educational life is questionable. However, at least the court allowed the McAdamses to try.

Annotated References and Resources

Constitutional and Statutory References

• The First Amendment to the Constitution provides that "Congress shall make no law respecting an establishment of religion, or prohibiting the free exercise thereof; or abridging the freedom of speech . . . ." The Fourteenth Amendment extended these prohibitions to apply also to the states.

• The Fourteenth Amendment to the Constitution prohibits the state from "depriv[ing] any person of life, liberty, or property, without due process;" or from "deny[ing] to any person within its jurisdiction the equal protection of the laws."

• Title VI of the Civil Rights Act of 1964, 42 U.S.C. § 2000 c, d, provides that "[n]o person in the United States shall, on the ground of race, color, or national origin, be excluded from participation in, be denied the benefits of, or be subjected to discrimination under any program or activity receiving Federal financial assistance." Section 601 of Title VI prohibits intentional discrimination based on race, color, or national origin in covered programs and activities. Section 602 authorizes federal agencies to effectuate Section 601 by issuing rules, regulations, or orders of general applicability that are consistent with achieving the objectives of the statute. The Supreme Court, in *Alexander v. Sandoval*, 532 U.S. 275 (2001), held that Congress intended to provide a private cause of action for individuals to enforce Section 601 (i.e., private individuals can sue in court for intentional discrimination). Section 602, however, does not provide a private right of action. Private individuals can go to court to seek redress only in cases alleging intentional racial discrimination. In cases where school practices or policies have a disparate impact on students of different races, parents can file a complaint with the Office for Civil Rights of the U.S. Department of Education. Information on filing a complaint is available at http://wdcrobcolp01.ed.gov/CFAPPS/OCR/contactus. cfm (accessed May 2004).

• Title IX of the Education Amendments of 1972, 20 U.S.C. § 1681, provides that "[n]o person . . . shall on the basis of sex, be excluded from participation in, be denied the benefits of, or be subjected to discrimination under any educational program or activity receiving Federal financial assistance."

• The Rehabilitation Act is 29 U.S.C. § 794. Section 504 of the Rehabilitation Act provides that students with disabilities receive educational support services.

- The Americans with Disabilities Act of 1990 (ADA), 42 U.S.C.A. § 12101, prohibits discrimination in employment against any "qualified individual with a disability." Coverage is not dependent upon an employer's receipt of federal funds.

- The Individuals with Disabilities Education Act (IDEA) is 20 U.S.C. § 1400, *et seq.*, as amended by Public Law 105-17 at 615 (I) (3) (A) 1997. IDEA authorizes "special education" services for students.

- Section 1983, Title 42 U.S.C. § 1983 states that "Every person who, under color of any statute, ordinance, regulation, custom, or usage, of any State or Territory or the District of Columbia, subjects or causes to be subjected, any citizen of the United States or other person within the jurisdiction thereof to the deprivation of any rights, privileges, or immunities secured by the Constitution and laws, shall be liable to the party injured in an action at law, suit in equity, or other proper proceeding for redress . . . ." Section 1983 provides a remedy for violations of constitutional rights or rights under federal law, and plaintiffs may plead complaints of Section 1983 violations simultaneously with allegations of discrimination prohibited by federal statutes such as Titles VI, VII, or IX; the Rehabilitation Act; or the Americans with Disabilities Act.

Court Decisions

- The two landmark Supreme Court desegregation decisions of the 1950s in which the Supreme Court ruled that, "in the field of public education, the doctrine of 'separate but equal' has no place," were *Brown v. Board of Education,* 347 U.S. 483 (1954) (Brown I), and *Brown v. Board of Education,* 349 U.S. 294 (1955) (Brown II). However, Supreme Court decisions beginning in the 1970s and continuing through the 1990s seemed aimed to temper the force of the *Brown* decisions, especially:

– *Milliken v. Bradley*, 418 U.S. 717 (1974),

– *Board of Education v. Dowell*, 498 U.S. 237 (1991),

– *Freeman v. Pitts*, 503 U.S. 467 (1992), and

– *Missouri v. Jenkins*, 515 U.S. 70 (1995).

Decisions Involving Racial Harassment

• Ray Jr.'s case is *Gant v. Wallingford Board of Education*, 195 F.3d 134 (2d Cir. 1999).

• Joshua Crispim's case is 2003 WL 21910698 (D. Conn.), from the federal district court in Connecticut. The "special relationship" legal theory was explained by the Supreme Court in *DeShaney v. Winnebago County Social Services Department*, 489 U.S. 189 (1989).

• The decision allowing a Title VI cause of action to proceed in the case brought by the Bryant brothers is *Bryant v. Independent School District No. I-38 of Garvin County, Oklahoma*, 334 F.3d 928 (10th Cir. 2003).

Decisions Involving Gender Orientation Harassment

• The Supreme Court in *Romer v. Evans*, 517 U.S. 620 (1996), affirmed a Colorado law designed to give homosexuals protection from discrimination based on their gender orientation, foreclosing the argument that homosexuals are not entitled to constitutional protection.

• One of the earliest cases of school district liability for not responding to gender orientation discrimination was *Nabozny v. Podlesny*, 92 F.3d 446 (7th Cir. 1996).

• Jesse Montgomery's case is *Montgomery v. Independent School District No. 709*, 109 F. Supp.2d 1081 (D. Minn. 2000).

• George Loomis' suit against the Visalia Unified School District is *Gay-Straight Alliance Network v. Visalia Unified School District*, 262 F. Supp.2d 1088 (E.D. Cal. 2001).

• Derek Henkle's lawsuit against the Washoe County School District in Nevada is *Henkle v. Gregory*, 150 F. Supp.2d 1067 (D. Nev. 2001).

• The community dispute in State College Area School District in Pennsylvania culminated in the lawsuit, *Saxe v. State College Area School District*, 240 F.3d 200 (3d Cir. 2001).

Decisions Involving Religion-Based Harassment

• The Satmar Hasidim's lawsuit is *Board of Education of Kiryas Joel Village School v. Grumet*, 114 S. Ct. 2481 (1994).

• Nicole Lindsley's suit against the Girard School District for religion-based harassment is *Lindsley v. Girard School District*, 213 F. Supp.2d 523 (W.D. Pa. 2002).

Decisions Involving Disability Harassment

• Arley McAdams' suit is *McAdams v. Board of Education of the Rocky Point Union Free School District*, 216 F. Supp.2d 86 (E.D.N.Y. 2002).

Journal Articles, Texts, and Commentaries

• For a discussion of the *Brown* decisions and subsequent cases diluting the force of those decisions, see Spital, S. (2003). Restoring *Brown's* promise of equality after *Alexander v. Sandoval*: Why we can't wait. *Harvard Blackletter Law Journal*, 19(93).

• The 2002 report of the Civil Rights Project at Harvard University (CRP) is McArdle, N., & Stuart, G. (2002). *Race, place, and segregation: Redrawing the color line in our nation's metros*. Cambridge, MA: The Civil Rights Project. The report is made up of four studies examining the change in the racial landscape of Boston, Chicago, and San Diego between 1990 and 2000. All four studies are available at www.civilrightsproject.harvard.edu/research/metro/three_metros.php. On April 21, 2004, the Metro Boston

Equity Initiative of the CRP released two new studies focused on the Boston area, demonstrating a strong correlation between racial segregation and diminished academic opportunity:

– Lee, C. (2004). *Racial segregation and educational outcomes in metropolitan Boston.* Cambridge, MA: The Civil Rights Project.
– Berger, J. B., Smith, S. M., & Coelen, S. P. (2004). *Race and the metropolitan origins of postsecondary access to four-year colleges: The case of greater Boston.* Cambridge, MA: The Civil Rights Project.

Both are available at www.civilrightsproject.harvard.edu (accessed May 2004).

• The settlements of George Loomis and David Henkle were reported in Walsh, M. (2002, September 4). Three districts pay damages in gay-rights lawsuits. *Education Week, 22*(1), 5.

• Thomas McLaughlin's settlement with the Pulaski County Special School District was reported in Trotter, A. (2003, July 19). Arkansas district settles lawsuit with gay student. *Education Week, 22*(43), 4.

• The Lambda Legal Defense Fund statistical sheet is Lambda Legal (2002). *Facts: Gay and lesbian youth in schools.* (Issued August 28, 2002). New York: Author. The document is available at www.lambdalegal.org/cgi-bin/iowa/documents/record?record= 1120 (accessed May 2004). The information in the document comes from the Office of Public Policy of the Gay, Lesbian and Straight Education Network (2001). *National school climate survey.* New York: Author. The network released a new survey in 2003, which is available at www.glsen.org/cgi-bin/iowa/all/news/record/ 1413.html (accessed May 2004). Also see:

– Bochenek, M., & Brown, A. W. (2001). *Hatred in the hallways: Violence and discrimination against lesbian, gay, bisexual, and transgender students in U.S. schools.* New York: Human Rights Watch. Available at www.hrw.org/reports/2001/uslgbt/ (accessed May 2004).

– Bowman, D. H. (2001, June 20). Report says schools often ignore harassment of gay students. *Education Week, 20*(39), 5.

• Information about the Harvey Milk School in New York and school admission policies is available at the Web site of the Hetrick-Martin Institute: www.hmi.org/Youth/HarveyMlkSchool/default. aspx (accessed May 2004).

• The dispute over the anti-harassment policy in the Westminster School District, Orange County, was reported in Zehr, M. A. (2004, March 24). Calif. board splits over gender identification. *Education Week, 23*(28), 5.

CHAPTER FIVE

Bullying and Harassment of Teachers and Other School Personnel

STUDENTS ARE NOT THE ONLY ONES WHO MAY FEEL BULLIED AND harassed in schools. Adults in the school setting are not immune to feelings of helplessness and victimization at the hands of bullies and harassers. Unfortunately, administrators, teachers, and other school personnel often feel like they are on the firing line, with volleys originating from one or more directions, sometimes simultaneously. Building principals may feel harassed by central office personnel: the superintendent or assistants, staff of buildings and grounds services, or even the transportation manager. At the same time, they may be receiving heat from disgruntled teachers or parents. Teachers may feel bullied or harassed by the building principal, as well as by students and their parents. Sometimes they receive parallel unfriendly fire from their peers.

Feelings of stress, unfortunately, are part and parcel of working in public education. The educational environment, with its high-stakes testing and pressures to meet the needs of children and parents with diverse backgrounds and expectations, can make even the most experienced educator feel bullied and harassed. However, sometimes educators experience bullying and harassment that produces more than "normal" stress. The bullying and harassment are not always about curriculum or the educational process.

Noneducational factors such as sex, gender orientation, race, age, and disability can also be at the root of bullying and harassment of educators, as well as of students.

Adults who feel they are being bullied or harassed in the school setting *should* take action to resolve the situation in adult ways: conferring with involved parties, bringing matters to the attention of disinterested supervisors, and employing conflict resolution skills. Of course, such platitudes are easy to offer. Administrators, teachers, and other school employees who feel they are being bullied or harassed in their workplace are often no more capable of resolving the situation in an "adult" manner than are their students. Persistent bullying and harassment can have that effect. Often, adults who are being bullied or harassed experience employment repercussions so severe that they feel their only recourse is to seek a remedy in law.

Title VII and Harassment

Title VII of the Civil Rights Act of 1964 is a federal statute closely related in both purpose and function to Titles VI and IX, the federal statutes discussed in relation to bullying and harassment of students. Title VII prohibits discrimination "against any individual with respect to his compensation, terms, conditions, or privileges of employment, because of such individual's race, color, religion, sex, or national origin." Individuals, however, cannot be held personally liable under Title VII, only employers, businesses, or corporations.

In a Title VII lawsuit, courts will often explicitly reference and apply what is known in legal circles as the "burden-shifting" paradigm set forth by the U.S. Supreme Court in 1973. Under this paradigm, the plaintiff must first establish a *prima facie* case of discrimination by showing a tangible, adverse employment action.

The employment action must be nontrivial, such as a hiring, discharge, compensation, or promotion decision. If the plaintiff succeeds in establishing a *prima facie* case, the burden then shifts to defendants to demonstrate a legitimate, nondiscriminatory reason for their action. If the defendants do so, the presumption of discrimination disappears, and the spotlight shifts back to the plaintiff, who then has a chance to show that the defendants' explanation was merely a fabrication or pretext for their real motive. The ultimate burden of proving discrimination rests with the plaintiff.

Most lawsuits alleging discrimination under Title VII involve sexual harassment in the workplace. Courts initially distinguished between two types of sexual harassment, *quid pro quo* and "hostile work environment" harassment, and apportioned liability depending on which form of sexual harassment the plaintiff alleged. Courts defined *quid pro quo* harassment as unwelcome sexual conduct that constituted a term of employment. "Have sex with me, or I'll have you fired" was a typical manifestation. If the employee established that *quid pro quo* sexual harassment had occurred, courts held the employer directly liable, and the harassed employee could recover monetary damages from the employer. Hostile work environment liability, on the other hand, was defined as unwelcome sexual conduct that unreasonably interfered with an employee's job performance or created an intimidating, hostile, or offensive work environment. Sexual jokes, "girlie" calendars picturing nude women or men, or uninvited advances could constitute a hostile work environment if sufficiently pervasive and persistent. Employers could be held vicariously liable for the existence of a hostile work environment or directly liable if an employee could show that the employer knew about the situation and did not take steps to correct the situation.

More recent court decisions have tended to ignore the distinctions between *quid pro quo* and hostile work environment harassment and have held employers blameworthy under Title VII if they have reason to know that an employee is being harassed in the workplace, whether based on race, religion, national origin, or sex, and do nothing about it. If the harassment is such that the employer could have prevented it by reasonable care in hiring, in supervising, or, if necessary, by firing the harasser, courts will hold the employer directly liable. Courts generally agree that Title VII is not designed to impose personal liability on individuals who perpetrate the harassment. Of course, companies typically have "deeper pockets" than do individuals, and litigants stand a better chance of recovering substantial monetary damages in establishing employer liability.

Because of the possibility of entity liability under Title VII, school districts generally take seriously their role in preventing sexual harassment of employees. Most districts have adopted anti-sexual harassment policies and provide mandatory sexual harassment training for employees. Such measures have not eradicated sexual harassment among adults in the public schools. The plaintiff's burden of proof in establishing school district liability for sexual harassment on the job, however, is high.

The *Alagna* Decision

The Eighth Circuit Court of Appeals issued a decision in April 2003 that exonerated the Smithville R-II School District in Missouri from liability for the claims of sexual harassment of a female guidance counselor by her male colleague. Kathy Alagna, the counselor, met David Yates, a science teacher at the school, when she interviewed him as part of her practicum for her master's degree in psychology in 1996. Two years later, Yates began calling Alagna at home, talking of his depression, suicidal thoughts, and marital problems. During the fall 1998 semester, Yates visited Alagna's guidance office two or three times per week, revealing intimate details of his personal life and touching her arm while saying he loved her, but stopping short of actually sexually propositioning her. Alagna reported Yates's conversations to her principal and eventually to the assistant superintendent, who was the district compliance coordinator for sexual harassment. The principal met with Yates and required him to attend a sexual harassment seminar.

Yates left Alagna alone for a while but resumed visiting her office in spring 1999. When Alagna reported these visits to the principal, the principal asked whether she could "imagine having sex with David Yates." Alagna interviewed and received offers for positions in other school districts, but she decided to stay at Smithville. The next year began no differently; Yates continued to tell Alagna he loved her, and Alagna began to feel a sexual overtone to Yates's attentions. She reported Yates to the principal again, and the principal gave Yates a second copy of the district's sexual harassment policy but did not direct him to stay away from Alagna. Alagna began locking her door, avoiding the school hallways and cafeteria, and carrying pepper spray. In January 2000, after Yates gave Alagna a wrapped gift that he asked her to open when she was alone, the principal finally directed Yates to stay away from Alagna. By then Alagna took an extended leave of absence from which she did not return.

After Alagna left, the assistant superintendent contacted her by letter to say he was "taking all measures short of termination" to stop Yates's unwelcome advances and asked her to respond. Alagna never did. The district offered her a position at the middle school, but she declined because she felt she should not have to leave the high school. Yates resigned effective the end of that school year, but Alagna still did not return to Smithville.

After Alagna filed suit alleging that the district violated Title VII by not dealing with the hostile work environment created by her colleague Yates, other teachers and students related that Yates had behaved in similar ways toward them, making statements of affection, brushing up against them, and invading their personal spaces. Yates also made telephone calls and visits to male teachers, expressing affection and giving them gifts.

The district court granted summary judgment to the school district, effectively stating that Alagna had no chance of winning the lawsuit under any legal theory. Alagna appealed. The Eighth Circuit Court of Appeals reviewed Alagna's burden under the law. To prove a claim of hostile work environment sexual harassment by a non-supervisory coworker, the court said, Alagna would have to show that

- she belonged to a protected group;
- she was subject to unwelcome sexual harassment;
- her harassment was based on sex;
- her harassment affected a term, condition, or privilege of employment; and
- her employer knew or should have known of the harassment and failed to take proper remedial action.

The district court had ruled that Alagna could not claim that Yates's unwelcome advances were based on her sex because he had behaved in similar inappropriate ways toward both females and males. Although making no comment on this "equal opportunity" harasser ruling, the court of appeals agreed with the district court that Alagna's harassment had not affected a term, condition, or privilege of her employment, because Yates's conduct had not risen to the requisite level of severity. To be actionable, the court said, the sexually harassing conduct must be "extreme," not merely rude or unpleasant. To affect a term, condition, or privilege of employment, the conduct must be frequent and severe; it must be physically threatening or humiliating. Yates, the court said, was merely "a troubled individual, insecure, depressed, and in need of constant reassurance of his worth as a human being." He was searching for friendship, not sex. Yates's conduct toward Alagna, the court concluded, did not create an objectively hostile work environment that was so intolerable that it would cause a reasonable person to resign. The unwritten court conclusion: Kathy Alagna was unreasonable in her reaction to the unwelcome attentions of her colleague David Yates.

What kinds of sexually explicit behaviors toward a female teacher would a court find sufficiently "extreme" as to create a truly hostile working environment? The court for Alagna's case cited behaviors such as "fondling his genitals in front of the victim," "intentionally brushing up against the victim's buttocks," "reference to a marker as 'big red penis,'" and "lewd jokes punctuated by gestures including touching breasts and thrusting hips." Are these behaviors objectively more "extreme" than constant telephoning, revealing intimate personal details of marital difficulties, and repeatedly visiting a private office to express "love"? A plaintiff cannot know in advance what a court will decide. Again, the burden of proving a viable Title VII claim is high.

Racial Harassment

Sexual harassment is not the only kind of harassment that can cause a teacher to feel victimized. Title VII also prohibits harassment because of race, color, or national origin. As the teaching staffs of public schools have become increasingly multicultural, teachers and administrators from foreign countries have had to contend with their communities' racial biases in their classrooms and school hallways. Sometimes that bias turns to bullying and harassment so daunting that teachers seek help in the courts.

A Teacher Prevails

Vincent Peries, a native of Sri Lanka, was academically highly qualified to teach in the New York City public school system. Educated in England, Peries continued his education in the United States after emigrating in 1968, earning a Ph.D. in adapted physical development and child development and degrees in international finance and teaching English as a second language. Peries taught at York College and New York University before joining the staff of Francis Lewis High School in Queens, New York, in 1987 as a special education teacher.

From the early 1990s, Peries experienced what he regarded as demeaning and insulting behavior based on his race by students and at least one of his colleagues. Between February 1996 and May 1997, he submitted verbal complaints and five written complaints about students mimicking his accent, calling him names like "Hindu" and "shit Indian," and telling him to "go home." Peries felt that the school administration did not treat his complaints or his situation seriously, putting the impossible burden of disciplining students back on him. Finally, in December 1997, Peries filed suit claiming that the district had violated Title VII and that several district administrators had violated his civil rights.

The district acknowledged that Peries had indeed been subjected to racial harassment by students but countered that its staff had acted by calling parents, reassigning students, and holding conferences. Because most of the offending students were special education students, the district argued, school officials were limited in the responses they could make to their harassing behavior.

The court noted that Peries's case was unusual because the typical Title VII lawsuit alleged the creation of a hostile work environment by coworkers and the toleration or encouragement of that environment by the employer. In this case, the offending parties were not district employees but students. The court looked to precedents in decisions involving claims of a hostile work environment in the commercial sector, where employees alleged that the actions of nonemployee customers had caused a hostile work environment. The degree of control that the employer is able to exercise over customers is dispositive, the court said.

Quoting *Davis v. Monroe County Board of Education*, the Supreme Court decision detailing a school district's responsibility in cases of student-on-student harassment, the court determined that school districts exercise substantial control over students who engage in harassing behavior in school. Whereas an individual teacher might be expected to exercise control over students, the court went on to say, school administrators not only are in greater positions of authority but also have a responsibility to teachers to exercise that authority.

The New York district court ruled that Peries had presented a sufficient showing of hostile work environment to entitle him to proceed with his suit. As part of proving his case and obtaining a judgment for damages, Peries would have to show the "severity of the abuse [he suffered], the nature of the humiliation, its interference with [his] teaching, and its effect on his psychological well-being." Whether the district would ultimately be held liable would depend on a jury's analysis of the actions the district took in response to Peries's complaints.

However, the court said, Peries could not hold the district administrators personally liable for violating his civil rights. District administrators were entitled to qualified immunity because no specific law requires that school administrators protect teachers from student-on-teacher harassment.

Peries and representatives of the school district were ordered to appear before the court for settlement discussions. As in many similar Title VII harassment suits, the legal record stops with the denial of summary judgment, when the court officially allows the plaintiff's lawsuit to proceed. Denial of a defendant's summary judgment motion often results in an offer of monetary settlement by the defendant. Unfortunately, the details of the settlement and the amount of any monetary damages are not part of the legal record. We can only speculate as to the final settlement in Peries's case.

A District Prevails

The U.S. Court of Appeals for the Seventh Circuit recently resolved a similar lawsuit alleging a hostile work environment because of student-on-teacher racial harassment in favor of the school district. The differences between the administrative responses to Peries's complaints and to those of Gema Salvadori, a Filipina science teacher in the Franklin (Wisconsin) School District, were significant, and they helped the court decide in favor of Franklin.

Salvadori filed her lawsuit when the school board discharged her after eight years of teaching science in the district. She charged that her dismissal was prompted by racial animus and in retaliation for her complaints about discriminatory practices tolerated by her school administration. Salvadori began her public school teaching assignment in Wisconsin at about the same time as Peries started his in New York, during the early 1990s. After six years of teaching science at the middle school with limited success in establishing student rapport or classroom management, Salvadori was transferred to the high school by the district for a fresh start. Students were rude to her there, asking whether she were an illegal alien, shouting at her to go back to the Philippines, throwing paper balls at her back, and referring to her with words like "bitch" and "fuck."

When she reported her complaints, however, unlike the weak response in Peries's case, the school administration took steps. The school principal, Dona Schwichtenberg, addressed the student body, making clear that the students' behavior was unacceptable and must stop. The principal and her assistants began monitoring the halls between classes to deter the harassment and to punish offenders. After receiving parent complaints about Salvadori's classroom management, Schwichtenberg tried to meet with Salvadori, but Salvadori ignored her. At the end of that year, the district terminated Salvadori's contract.

In analyzing Salvadori's complaints, the Seventh Circuit acknowledged an employer's duty to take reasonable steps to discover and rectify acts of harassment toward employees. That duty, the court said, is more difficult in a high school full of "pumped-up teenagers." However, the court recognized the "reasonable and swift" action of the principal in addressing the student body and prohibiting the offensive conduct and her action with her associates in patrolling the school hallways in response to the harassment. These simple actions helped convince the court to rule in favor of the Franklin School District's motion for summary judgment, thereby deciding that Gema Salvadori had no legal basis on which she could prevail.

An Administrator's Lawsuit

Teachers are not the only ones who allege racial discrimination when challenging district employment decisions. African American assistant principal DeComa Love-Lane filed suit alleging that her superintendent and the Winston-Salem/Forsyth County Board of Education had discriminated against her because of race in violation of Title VII when they refused to renew her administrative contract and reassigned her to a teaching position in the district. Love-Lane asserted that the board's action was in retaliation for her stance opposing what she characterized as racially discriminatory practices in the district, especially the establishment of her school's time-out room, an in-school suspension room to which more black students than white were assigned. However, other conflicts within the purview of Love-Lane's duty assignment were documented, such as unprofessional communications and manners in meetings, refusal to accept professional criticism, and attempts to undermine teachers' relationships with parents.

The U.S. District Court in North Carolina applied the burden-shifting paradigm often used in Title VII lawsuits. The court found that the assistant principal had failed to establish a *prima facie* case of discrimination because Love-Lane had not been performing satisfactorily at the time the board refused to renew her administrative contract but instead reassigned her to the classroom. Numerous district performance evaluations and the testimony of Love-Lane's colleagues and supervisors established that she was difficult to deal with, unprofessional in her district interactions, and obstructive at the time of her contract nonrenewal and reassignment.

Satisfactory performance at the time when an adverse employment decision is made is critical to a plaintiff's case. If an administrator, teacher, or any other school employee is not performing her job in a satisfactory manner at the time an adverse employment decision is made, she strikes out. One of the most effective ways a district can forestall a Title VII lawsuit is to keep factual, accurate, contemporaneous, and complete performance records and evaluations for administrators, teachers, and all other district employees.

A Reverse Discrimination Lawsuit

In an interesting and long-drawn-out twist on usual race discrimination cases, two Caucasian Rochester City School District teachers sued the district alleging racial discrimination by predominantly white administrators of the district in violation of Title VII. Richard Seils and Lois Vreeland filed suit alleging breach of contract, racial discrimination, retaliation, and violation of civil rights in a lengthy and repetitive set of complaints and pleadings that the court analogized to the "tortured procedural history" of the *Jarndyce v. Jarndyce* litigation portrayed by Charles Dickens in *Bleak House*. Fifty-nine-year-old Seils also alleged age discrimination under the Americans with Disabilities Act. Vreeland's claims were so unclear that the court noted that she appeared to claim harassment by students because of race, gender, age, disability, marital status, and her mixed-race children. That the court would grant summary judgment was evident from the first paragraphs of the decision, but the court's analysis is complete and instructive.

Discrimination that disadvantages any race, Caucasian, African American, or other, is prohibited by Title VII, without exception. In reverse discrimination cases, the same standards apply: the plaintiff must show that (1) he is a member of the racial minority, (2) he was performing satisfactorily, (3) he suffered some adverse employment action, and (4) such action occurred under circumstances giving rise to an inference of discrimination. Just because all or most of the administrators in a school district are the same race as plaintiffs does not necessarily negate an inference of discrimination, but, the court noted, only a "most unusual" employer would choose to discriminate against the majority. Ultimately, the court ruled that neither Seils nor Vreeland carried the burden of demonstrating that either of them had received less favorable treatment than similarly situated colleagues. They alleged that the district had failed to help them surmount difficult classroom management situations, but district administrators had disciplined their disruptive students in the same way they dealt with all similar student offenders: the administration suspended offending students, segregated others from the complaining teacher, and transferred others. Underneath the court's analysis seem to run an acknowledgment and acceptance that school administrators cannot cure all classroom ills, that administrators can only do their best to support classroom discipline and rely on teachers to do likewise. Administrators' failure to cure negative situations is not discrimination.

Gender Orientation Discrimination

With the increasing openness and acceptance of gays and lesbians in professional and nonprofessional positions in school districts, more employee lawsuits alleging discrimination based on gender orientation or gender choice are appearing. *Education Week* (Walsh, 2002) reports that, in addition to the large monetary settlements several school districts had paid to gay students harassed by peers and teachers, a heterosexual English teacher, Karl Debro, in San Leandro, California, received a $1.2 million settlement to end his lawsuit against the district after the district had disciplined him for discussing gay rights and minority issues with students. The jury also awarded Debro $500,000 for emotional distress. Debro's case underscores the sensitive nature of the gender orientation issue in schools.

Although Title VII says nothing about discrimination based on sexual orientation, the Fourteenth Amendment guarantees every person, regardless of sexual orientation, the equal protection of the law. Administrators, teachers, and other school employees who feel that the school district has denied them equal protection by failing to protect them from harassment based on their sexual orientation can bring a cause of action under Section 1983 of the Civil Rights Act of 1964. As in sexual harassment cases, whether they will be successful depends at least in part on the school district's responses to their allegations.

Illustrative of how courts will analyze claims of deprivation of civil rights for failure to protect from sexual orientation harassment is the Seventh Circuit Court of Appeals decision in a lawsuit brought by Tommy R. Schroeder, a teacher for 15 years in the Hamilton School District in Wisconsin. Shortly after moving to Templeton Middle School, Schroeder disclosed his homosexuality to several colleagues and subsequently at a public meeting.

In 1993–1994, Schroeder began experiencing harassment based on his sexual orientation, primarily from students who repeatedly called him a "faggot," accused him of having AIDS, and scrawled obscenities about his sex life on bathroom walls. Administrators attempted to discipline the offending students, but much of the harassment was anonymous, and the associate principal discussed with Schroeder how difficult it was to identify the perpetrators and discipline them. Schroeder wanted school officials to conduct schoolwide sensitivity training and felt that administrators did not pursue sexual orientation harassment with the same vigor as they did racial harassment.

Finally, after several years, Schroeder received a transfer to the elementary level where he taught 1st and 2nd grade students. The harassment continued, this time primarily at the hands of adults, presumably school parents. Parents removed their children from his class, spread rumors that he was a pedophile, made anonymous harassing telephone calls, and slashed his car tires. In February 1998, Schroeder had a mental breakdown and resigned from his teaching position; he applied for and received disability benefits for the rest of the school year. In June 1999, the district terminated Schroeder's employment.

Schroeder sued the school district, alleging that by failing to protect him from sexual orientation harassment, the district had violated his Section 1983 right to equal protection under the law. He essentially argued that the district had treated him differently because of his homosexuality.

The court noted that because homosexuals do not enjoy heightened protections under the law as do members of minority groups or females, the court is not required to analyze discrimination toward homosexuals as stringently as it would for a protected group. "A plaintiff must demonstrate intentional or purposeful discrimination to show an equal protection violation" under Section

1983, the court stated. Moreover, the court would not allow Schroeder to create a right to a Title VII cause of action through a Section 1983 argument.

According to the court, the Hamilton School District did not intentionally discriminate against Tommy Schroeder. Merely failing to hold the gender orientation sensitivity training that Schroeder requested, or failing to act on his complaints of homosexual harassment as forcefully as they addressed racial discrimination, did not amount to intentional discrimination. School districts, the court admonished, have limited resources and must prioritize their use of time and resources in favor of students' needs. "Furthermore, in a school setting, the well-being of students, not teachers, must be the primary concern of school administrators," the court continued. Schools cannot use police tactics to deal with nonviolent harassment of a teacher by students, the Seventh Circuit concluded, even if the harassment is cruel and offends. Schools can teach students to be civil, but they cannot control parents unless parents are on school grounds, and they can do little to curb anonymous actions that harass and annoy an individual teacher. In finally denying Schroeder's pleadings and granting summary judgment to the school district, the Seventh Circuit exhorted judges to refrain from using the courts to impose their own social values on public school administrators "who already have innumerable obstacles to face."

The U.S. District Court for the Eastern District of New York reached an opposite conclusion when a homosexual female teacher brought a Section 1983 cause of action against her school district, alleging that the district had violated her right to equal protection of the laws because it had failed to protect her from harassment.

Like Tommy Schroeder, Joan Lovell accused her district of handling her complaints of sexual orientation harassment less seriously and less effectively than other teachers' similar allegations of racial harassment. The district moved to dismiss her claim entirely.

The court stated the applicable standard of review for a defendant's motion to dismiss: A court may grant the motion only if it appears beyond doubt that the plaintiff has no legal argument that would support a decision in her favor. The court must examine the facts stated in the plaintiff's complaint, in documents submitted by the plaintiff in support of her complaint, and in matters of which judicial notice may be taken (e.g., information available in reputable publications or governmental statistics). Not only did the court refuse to dismiss Joan Lovell's claim, the court ruled that Lovell's principal had likely violated her Fourteenth Amendment right to equal protection by treating her differently than he would have treated a similarly situated non-lesbian teacher. Moreover, the court said, the actions of the principal as head of the school represented official school district policy. Since an employee's right to equal treatment under the law was well established, the court continued, neither the principal nor the school district could affirmatively claim qualified immunity as a defense to the treatment accorded Lovell.

A 27-year veteran of the school district, Lovell began having difficulties when three female students in her art class went to the principal with sexual harassment complaints against her. Although Lovell had been in the school office shortly after the students had lodged their complaints, the principal did not inform Lovell of the complaints, as school policy required. Instead, the principal gave one of the students a pass to leave Lovell's class at any time. When Lovell went to inquire about the pass near the end of the school day, the assistant principal informed her of the complaints.

In her suit, Lovell contended that the students who lodged the complaints were behavior problems in her classroom, and that one who was failing the course had insisted that she was "going to get out of" the class. She did so grandly, because the principal unilaterally removed the failing student and ultimately rewarded her with a grade of 100 percent for an "independent study" project. After the principal's action, the three students began to harass Lovell, calling her a "dyke" and hugging themselves when they saw Lovell in the school hallways. The school took no action to punish the students.

Though the court record does not indicate what monetary damages, if any, Lovell ultimately received, the court's strongly worded refusal to consider any possible defense for the administrative inaction in the face of Lovell's harassment signifies for school administrators the absolute necessity of treating *all* harassment of teachers according to the same established policy and practice, no matter what the sexual preference of the individual. School administrators also must respect the rights of all teachers to be advised of student complaints that potentially affect their professional reputations. Otherwise, allegations of different treatment based on characteristics that do not strictly implicate professional competence may cost the district in terms of legal fees and negative publicity, even if the allegations are ultimately dismissed.

Annotated References and Resources

Court Decisions

• The Supreme Court, in *Meritor Savings Bank v. Vinson,* 477 U.S. 57 (1986) and *Harris v. Forklift Systems, Inc.,* 510 U.S. 17 (1993), ruled that sexual harassment is a form of sex discrimination prohibited under Title VII of the Civil Rights Act of 1964, 42 U.S.C. § 2000 e. Individuals, however, cannot be held personally liable under Title VII. Individuals can be held liable, however, under a Section 1983 claim of deprivation of the rights to due process and equal protection under the Fourteenth Amendment that prohibits the state from "depriv[ing] any person of life, liberty, or property, without due process;" or from "deny[ing] to any person within its jurisdiction the equal protection of the laws." School districts and school boards are local government entities that can be held liable under Section 1983, but only if they establish an official policy, or tolerate a custom or practice, that leads to, causes, or results in the deprivation of a constitutionally protected right. (*Monell v. Department of Social Services*, 436 U.S. 58 (1978)). The "toleration" can be inaction in the face of repeated notification of problems, as in *Massey v. Akron City Board of Education*, 82 F. Supp.2d 735 (N.D. Ohio, 2000). School district employees, like principals and teachers, are liable as individual state actors under Section 1983.

• The "burden-shifting" paradigm used in Title VII analysis was enunciated by the Supreme Court in *McDonnell Douglas Corporation v. Green*, 411 U.S. 792 (1973).

• Kathy Alagna's case is *Alagna v. Smithville R-II School District*, 324 F.3d 975 (8th Cir. 2003).

• Vincent Peries's case is *Peries v. New York City Board of Education*, 2001 WL 1328921 (E.D.N.Y.), a case of first impression in which the court cited to *Quinn v. Green Tree Credit Corporation*, 159 F.3d 759 (2d Cir. 1998), for the proposition that the duty of an employer with respect to sexual harassment by a non-employee customer cannot be greater than the duty owed with respect to coworker harassment, and to *Davis v. Monroe County Board of Education*, 526 U.S. 629 (1999) to reiterate the degree of control a school district is expected to exercise over students.

• Gema Salvadori's case is *Salvadori v. Franklin School District*, 293 F.3d 989 (7th Cir. 2002).

• DeComa Love-Lane's suit is *Love-Lane v. Martin*, 201 F. Supp.2d 566 (M.D.N.C. 2002).

• Richard Seils and Lois Vreeland attempted to sue the Rochester City School District in *Seils v. Rochester City School District*, 192 F. Supp.2d 100 (W.D.N.Y. 2002).

• Tommy Schroeder's case is *Schroeder v. Hamilton School District*, 282 F.3d 946 (7th Cir. 2002). The court subsequently denied a motion by Schroeder's counsel for a rehearing of the case by all the justices of the Seventh Circuit sitting *en banc*, that is, as a whole.

• Joan Lovell's case is *Lovell v. Comsewogue School District*, 214 F. Supp.2d 319 (E.D.N.Y.2002).

Journal Articles, Texts, and Commentaries

• The monetary awards to Karl Debro are reported in Walsh, M. (2002, September 4). Three districts pay damages in gay-rights lawsuits. *Education Week*, 22(1), 5. The same article reported monetary awards to students George Loomis and David Henkle.

CHAPTER SIX

Student Threats and Violence in Schools

ALTHOUGH MANY EDUCATORS MAY FEEL HARD-PRESSED TO DEFINE A "threat," most are confident that they would recognize one when it occurs. Problems often arise, however, when school personnel try to take legal action against students whom they perceive as making threats to harm others. A student who uses what appears to be threatening language simply may be exercising a First Amendment right to express an opinion, a right protected from governmental interference or suppression, even in the school setting. Under the United States legal system, what a reasonable educator might categorize as a threat may or not be a "true threat" under the law.

At a Washington, D.C., political rally in August 1966, an 18-year-old unhappy with his 1-A draft classification declared, "If they ever make me carry a rifle, the first man I want to get in my sights is LBJ," referring to then-President Lyndon B. Johnson. The young man, Robert Watts, was charged with and convicted of a felony under a federal statute that makes it a crime to "willfully and knowingly" threaten the president. The U.S. Supreme Court reversed his conviction three years later in what became the seminal Court decision distinguishing between threats and "true threats." Recognizing a "profound national commitment to . . . debate on public issues," including speech that may be "vehement, caustic, and unpleasantly sharp," the Court found that the youth's statement was merely "political hyperbole." Watts, the Court decided, had not uttered a true threat. Unfortunately, the Supreme Court declined to help educators by explaining what would make ordinary threatening-sounding words into a true threat.

Deciding What Constitutes a True Threat

Fast-forward to February 1993. Sarah Lovell, a 15-year-old California high school student, has been trying all day to get her class schedule changed. She has been shuffled back and forth between the assistant principal's and guidance offices. Finally, she thinks her schedule is settled, but when Linda Suokko, her guidance counselor, enters the changes into the master schedule, Suokko sees that the assistant principal has approved Sarah for courses that are already overloaded. Suokko tells the girl that she may not be able to make the changes. Sarah loses her patience and, according to Suokko, says, "If you don't give me this schedule change, I'm going to shoot you." Although Sarah apologizes immediately and insists that she did not say those exact words, her principal suspends her and files a strongly worded student referral form as part of her permanent record.

When Sarah's parents brought suit to have the referral form removed from her file, the Court of Appeals for the Ninth Circuit upheld the principal's actions, ruling that Sarah's communication to Suokko was a "true threat." Alleged threats, according to the Ninth Circuit, are judged by an objective standard that focuses on the speaker. The test is whether a reasonable person uttering a communication would foresee that the listener would interpret the statement as a serious expression of intent to harm. True threats, the Ninth Circuit emphasized, are not among the categories of expression protected by the First Amendment. Sarah's principal, therefore, was justified in suspending Sarah and filing the student referral form. In addition to the "objective speaker" test, the Ninth Circuit also requires that statements appearing to be threats "should be considered in light of their entire factual context." If the words uttered and the surrounding circumstances are so "unequivocal, unconditional, immediate, and specific" that they convey a seriousness of purpose and the prospect of being carried out in the near future, then the statement is a true threat.

Courts in the Ninth Circuit, then, like Sarah Lovell's court, will rule that a putative threatening statement is a true threat if the speaker, as a reasonable person, should have foreseen that the listener would interpret the statement uttered as a threat of bodily harm or assault. The burden is on the speaker to reasonably foresee an unpleasant reaction to what was said, considering all the circumstances. Sarah, as a reasonable person, should have known her statement would upset Suokko. The Ninth Circuit's definition of true threat says nothing about how reasonable the *listener* must be. Suokko could have completely overreacted to Sarah's words; in fact, she may even have misheard the student. Practically speaking, the Ninth Circuit requires speakers to know in advance their listeners' reactions. Moreover, using the Ninth Circuit's reasonable speaker standard, one wonders whether a frustrated teenager in Sarah's circumstances could ever be considered reasonable.

If Sarah Lovell had expressed her frustration in another state—for example, in Virginia or Maryland, both of which are bound by the standards adopted by the Fourth Circuit Court of Appeals—the standard that the court applied would have been different. Courts in the Fourth Circuit judge whether a communication is a true threat solely by considering the communication's effect on the recipient. Whether or not the speaker had any idea, or even considered, how the listener would react to her allegedly threatening communication is unimportant in complaints litigated in Virginia or Maryland.

This point may not have made a difference in Sarah's case, because Suokko, the listener, also perceived Sarah's words as a threat. Nevertheless, the judicial standards in many states are different and have different implications. Focusing solely on the listener's reaction may negate totally consideration of the speaker's intent in the communication. Focusing solely on what a speaker should have known in advance about the listener's reaction presumes that the speaker was capable of rational thought when she may have been completely consumed by anger or frustration. Deciding whether a communication is a true threat that is actionable under the law, therefore, depends on the analysis adopted by the relevant jurisdiction.

Threats Delivered in Different Forms

In addition to speaker and listener tests, other jurisdictions have adopted hybrid tests or burdened traditional tests with specific requirements (e.g., that the threat be directly communicated to the intended victim). Technology that facilitates communication at a distance complicates the analysis. For example, either party to a telephone conversation may misperceive communications, because the speaker and listener can only hear each other but not distinguish visual cues. Similarly, nonverbal modes of communication, like works of art, confound traditional true threat analyses. Poetry may do the same.

E-Mail Threats

Internet communication is even more problematic. In the Sixth District in Michigan, for example, true threat analysis requires that the speaker have the intent to intimidate the recipient of the communication and that the alleged threat be communicated directly to the intended victim in some way. The Sixth Circuit applied this analysis to a series of Internet communications sent by a University of Michigan student to a chat room friend in Canada. In his messages, the student, who used the name "Jake Baker," expressed his intent to rape and sodomize young girls and women. Baker attracted the Canadian's attention through a series of sexually violent stories he had posted to an interactive Usenet bulletin board, in which he described the rape, mutilation, and murder of women and young girls.

From November 1994 until January 1995, Baker and his new online friend, known only as Arthur Gonda, exchanged e-mail messages discussing sexual violence that they hoped to inflict on women. On January 9, 1995, Baker publicly disseminated via the bulletin board a story in which he specifically identified by name a female fellow undergraduate at the University of Michigan, and described in horrific graphic detail how he would torture, rape, and murder her. An alarmed citizen who encountered Baker's posting notified University of Michigan authorities. When questioned by university personnel, the young woman appeared so emotionally traumatized that the university recommended psychological counseling. (All official records refer to her simply as "Jane Doe.") The Federal Bureau of Investigation (FBI) subsequently filed a complaint against Baker, whose real name was actually Abraham Jacob Alkabaz, and a grand jury indicted him for violation of 18 U.S.C. § 875, a federal statute criminalizing interstate communications containing threats to kidnap or injure another person.

The district court in Michigan dismissed the indictment, holding that the communications were not true threats. The prosecution appealed to the Sixth Circuit Court of Appeals. A panel of three judges heard the appeal, and agreed with the district court, ruling two-to-one that Baker's communications were not true threats. In the published decision, Boyce F. Martin, Jr., chief judge, engaged in an extended discussion of the nature of threats, stating,

"At their core, threats are tools that are employed when one wishes to have some effect, or achieve some goal, through intimidation." Baker's communications, Martin wrote, were not intended to intimidate; they were never even communicated directly to his classmate. Therefore, they were not true threats. Baker and his Canadian friend, Martin continued, were simply attempting "to foster a friendship based on shared sexual fantasies." Martin's colleague on the bench, Judge Robert Krupansky, vigorously dissented, defining a threat in a more familiar way, as a "simple, credible declaration of an intent to cause injury to some person." However, "Jake Baker" went free. The court decision remains as only one of many adding to the confusion as to what constitutes a true threat under the law.

Would K–12 students ever engage in the kind of online communications published by Jake Baker? Public school districts that provide e-mail privileges to students and school personnel undoubtedly employ acceptable-use policies to put them on notice of what constitutes appropriate e-mail communication. When students and staff are aware of their diminished expectations of privacy in e-mail communications, most self-monitor their online speech. However, many students erroneously believe that the anonymity of the Internet protects them. In 2000, the Boston public school system ended free Hotmail and Yahoo e-mail accounts for students after two boys at the Boston Arts Academy had sent threatening e-mails to a female classmate who refused to date them. The district subsequently installed e-mail accounts that can be immediately traced back to the sender. That same year, a Florida teenager was sentenced to prison after he had sent an e-mail message to a Columbine High School sophomore, threatening to "finish Columbine."

Threatening Songs

As the Florida case demonstrates, technology-assisted communication can certainly count as a true threat. But can "entertainment" be a threat? Can a student-created rap song be a true threat? Does the song have to be recognizable as a song?

An Arkansas junior high school student intended to write a violent rap song in the style of Eminem and other controversial rappers after his girlfriend broke up with him. The student, however, seemed to lack musical talent, and his song had no discernible beat or rhythm. What his writings did contain, however, were violent rantings about how he wanted to molest, rape, and murder his former girlfriend. He never delivered the purported lyrics but instead left them on his bedroom dresser. A classmate discovered them weeks later and read them. Some time after this, the girlfriend found out about the "song." She arranged with the friend who had read the papers to steal them for her, and she read them in gym class. A student who observed her reading them noticed her very apparent distress and reported the threatening letter to the school security officer.

The principal subsequently suspended the would-be rapper for the remainder of his 8th grade year. The student's mother brought a lawsuit against the school district, suing for his reinstatement. The Arkansas court, acknowledging that courts in the Eighth Circuit where the state is located use a reasonable listener standard to analyze true threats, declined to use the traditional test. Instead, the court decided to apply the reasonable *speaker* test used in Sarah Lovell's case. In reality, however, they applied an amalgam of speaker and listener standards to decide that the feeble rap song was a true threat. The court also explicitly noted that in the wake of Jonesboro and Columbine, any reasonable school official would have taken action based on the content of the young man's papers.

This rap song case is especially interesting because the Court of Appeals, in a first sitting, decided that the song was protected speech. Courts of Appeals usually sit as a body of three judges to hear a case. After the decision of the three-judge panel in this case, the entire case was reheard *en banc* (i.e., by all the judges of the court sitting together). The full court came to its final decision, that the 8th grader's rap song was a true threat, by a narrow margin, and the decision contains four sharply divided dissenting opinions.

Another Arkansas court dealing with an allegedly threatening rap song also ruled that the song in question was a true threat. In this case, the rapper was a 15-year-old student who had become angry when his female classmate and former friend snubbed him. He wrote, "I'll murder you before you can think twice, cut you up and use you for decoration to look nice." The writer had a record of juvenile arrests, and the fellow student whom the rapper threatened knew of this record and believed that he would carry out the threats. Although the rapper argued to the court that he was exercising his First Amendment right to free speech when he wrote the song, the court ruled that, as a true threat, the words fell outside the protection of the First Amendment.

Poetry and Art as Threats

Two other cases from California illustrate the difficulty educators may have in recognizing a true threat when the alleged threat is not delivered in a spoken, face-to-face context. Both cases were brought to court as violations of the same California statute criminalizing true threats, a statute containing very specific and unambiguous language. In one, a male high school student nicknamed Julius, new to the school, gave a handwritten note containing "dark poetry," which warned that he could be "the next kid to bring guns to kill students at school," to at least two different female classmates from his honors English class. In the other case, another male high school student, Ryan D., turned in for credit for his art class a realistic painting depicting the execution by gunshot of a police officer who had recently "busted" him for marijuana possession.

The California statute criminalizing true threats, Penal Code § 422, requires that the prosecution establish that the accused willfully threatened to commit a crime that would result in death or great bodily injury to another person. Under the statute, the prosecution does not have to show that the accused threat-maker actually had the intent to *carry out* the threat but simply that the threat was made with the specific intent it be taken as a threat. In addition, the California statute tracks the language of several Supreme Court decisions and requires that the threat, either standing alone or considering the surrounding circumstances, be so "unequivocal, unconditional, immediate, and specific" that it conveys to the threatened person a gravity of purpose and immediate prospect of its being carried out. Finally, the threat must have reasonably caused the threatened person to be in sustained fear of harm.

Applying the same statute to both the would-be poet and the aspiring artist resulted in two different outcomes: the poet was convicted of making a true threat, and the artist was let off. Why did these two cases come out differently?

The courts in both cases looked at not only the actual threats—the words of the poem or the painting itself—but also the circumstances surrounding each. In Julius's case, he was the "new kid" in school; he had been thrown out of two other high schools in the district for offenses other than threats: urinating on the wall and plagiarism. Evidence showed that he and his father were living with his uncle, who owned a stash of rifles and guns that Julius had discovered. Julius did not really know the girls to whom he showed his poems, and his class was not studying or discussing poetry at the time he divulged his works. Although Julius asserted that he was writing the poems as a fictional character, the court took into consideration his admitted feelings that the district was "out to get him," and it ruled that his poems had been intended as a threat to get back at the district by terrorizing innocent students.

Could Julius simply have been a lonely student, reaching out to his classmates for acceptance by offering them his poems? One of his poems had written at the top of the page, "These poems describe me and my feelings. Tell me if they describe you and your feelings." The dissenting judge, at least, thought so and noted that Julius's poem said he *could* be the next to bring guns to school, not that he *would*. The majority found the distinction not significant, focusing instead on the sustained fear that Julius's poems inspired in his female classmates.

In Ryan D.'s case, the court also examined the circumstances surrounding his painting. The officer was readily identifiable as Ryan's arresting officer in his marijuana conviction—her badge number was clearly depicted. Although Ryan admitted that he was angry at the police officer for arresting him and had painted the graphic shooting scene to show his anger, knowing the officer would see the painting, the court found it relevant that Ryan had handed in the painting for a class grade. Despite the testimony of the arresting officer that she considered the painting to be a threat, the court decided that Ryan's submission of the painting for class credit resolved the "ambiguous" intent of the expression; the painting was not a true threat.

How would another set of judges rule on the same facts? Did Julius "look like" a terrorist, and did Ryan look like a clean-cut kid? Are words more forceful than painted images? These two judicial rulings, from the same California jurisdiction and based on the same California statute, centered on similar imagery of bodily harm and death, arrive at opposite conclusions. They now serve as either controlling or persuasive authority for the next cases involving threatening expression, and lawyers for either side can argue opposite outcomes justified by precedent.

No Threat if Classroom Assignment

In Ryan D.'s case, the court made much of the fact that Ryan had turned in his graphic painting as a class assignment for an art grade. Does the fact that a student's allegedly threatening communication comes in the context of an actual school assignment mitigate the force of a threat? An 8th grade student in a creative writing class was found delinquent after he wrote a composition about concealing a machete and chopping off his English teacher's head. Although the student, Douglas D., specifically named the teacher in his writing and wrote the assignment after being disciplined and sent out of the classroom to a seat in the hallway, the Supreme Court of Wisconsin reversed his delinquency adjudication, ruling that his composition did not constitute a true threat. The court recognized a need for "more creative license" in a creative writing class than in, say, a math class. For instance, Douglas wrote his story in the third person; it also attempted at jest, the court said, when Douglas penned that the teacher's name, Mrs. C., stood for Mrs. Crab. Besides, the court said, a story about killing with a machete was unrealistic and not to be taken seriously.

Was Douglas really threatening Mrs. C.? Mrs. C. was a first-year teacher. She testified that she felt panicked by Douglas's composition. She had had discipline problems with Douglas before this incident. Douglas was not a model student; he had a pattern of delinquency and skipping school. The record showed that he was "a troubled young man." Yet the court decided that Douglas was not making a true threat against Mrs. C. The school, the court said, still had the right to discipline Douglas for violation of the student rules of conduct, but the First Amendment protected Douglas's right to speak freely and graphically in his composition.

Bomb Threats

Bomb threats, even if groundless or pranks, seriously disrupt the ongoing operations of schools. Besides instilling fear and forcing cancellation of classes and building closures, such threats also cost school districts considerable funds to install telephone systems to trace calls and video cameras to monitor nonclassroom areas of buildings, to investigate and prosecute perpetrators, and to hire extra personnel to observe student activities effectively. Many school districts specifically mention making terroristic threats as an actionable offense in their student codes of conduct. All states have adopted laws making it a crime to communicate a bomb threat to a school, even if the perpetrator knows the threat is untrue, and school districts have begun to cooperate vigorously with law enforcement authorities in prosecuting guilty students. However, schools need to exercise care in alerting authorities and charging students with making terroristic threats. Bomb threats are serious business and carry serious consequences under the law; these consequences need to be applied only to prosecute students who truly deserve prosecution.

For example, Jason W. did not need to be prosecuted. Jason was a middle school student at Clear Spring Middle School in Washington County, Maryland, on December 13, 2001. At 9:15 a.m., a teacher found him scribbling with a pencil on the wall near a school stairway. It appeared he had written "There is a bomb," but when the teacher spied him, he began erasing the word "bomb." The teacher took Jason to the school principal.

The principal obviously did not take Jason's threat seriously. He did not evacuate the school building; he did not notify the fire marshal or call in bomb detection or disposal agencies. The normal operations of the school were not disrupted. In fact, no one even took a photograph of Jason's writing, which, after his furious erasing, ended in an illegible smudge.

However, the school contacted law enforcement authorities, who brought charges against Jason. Communicating a false bomb threat in Maryland is a felony. Even if Jason had been convicted of "disturbing . . . the orderly conduct of schools," a misdemeanor, he could have received a six-month jail sentence and a $3,500 fine. As it was, the court adjudicated him as a delinquent.

Jason's parents appealed. The Court of Special Appeals found that Jason's wall writing had not disturbed the normal operations of the school. The court said that the lower court's reading of the statute raised the "specter of a young child being hauled into juvenile court and found delinquent for throwing a temper tantrum in school . . . . Disruptions of one kind or another no doubt occur every day in the schools," the court continued, and "there is a level of disturbance that is simply part of the school activity." Jason was off the hook, and the school district was publicly admonished.

Threats to Harm Self

Schools are supposed to be places where children and teenagers can learn without fearing for their safety. When students make threatening statements directed at members of the school community, school officials are usually quick to react. But what about a student's threat to harm himself? Does the school have a duty to protect students from themselves? Do guidance counselors, teachers, or other school personnel have a legal duty to warn parents that they suspect a student intends self-harm or suicide?

More than 25 years ago, the California Supreme Court imposed a much-debated "duty to warn" on therapists who learn that their patients intend harm to another. The litigation arose after a University of California at Berkeley student, Prosenjit Poddar, told his university hospital psychotherapist that he intended to kill his former girlfriend, Tatiana Tarasoff. Poddar actually carried out his threat. Tarasoff's parents sued the regents of the University of California, the hospital's psychotherapists, and the university police for failing to protect their daughter. The court ruled that once a therapist determines that a serious threat of violence to another exists, he or she has a duty to "exercise reasonable care to protect the foreseeable victim." This duty to warn foreseeable victims of harm, now called the "*Tarasoff* duty," has been adopted in several states and extended to apply not only to therapists but also to many other professionals who engage in confidential relationships with clients.

Should the law recognize a *Tarasoff*-kind of duty for educators who receive student confidences threatening suicide? Where a duty exists, the potential for liability also exists. Should educators and their school districts be held liable for failing to prevent student suicides whose warning signs were, or should have been, apparent? Many surviving parents, believing they should, have pursued remedies through the courts.

Suicide in Schools

More people die from suicide than from homicides, according to the Centers for Disease Control (2000). Many of these suicide victims are young people. Between 1981 and 1998, the Office of Juvenile Justice and Delinquency Prevention reports, 20,775 juveniles ages 7–17 committed suicide in the United States. Of these juvenile suicides, 62 percent were committed with a firearm. The states with the highest juvenile suicide rates were Alaska, Montana, Idaho, Wyoming, and New Mexico, in that order (Snyder & Swahn, 2004).

Even more alarming than the overall numbers of student suicides is the increase in the suicide rate among middle school students, a rate that has increased more than 100 percent over the last decade. Among 13- and 14-year-olds, as many youngsters committed suicide as were murdered. While suicides among white males still predominate, rates for minority students are increasing. Suicide rates for black male adolescents as a group increased 240 percent between 1981 and 1998 (Snyder & Swahn, 2004). Black males ages 15–24 showed the greatest increase in suicide completion rates in the 1990s compared with other minority groups. In addition, gay and lesbian adolescents were 200–300 percent more likely to attempt suicide than other young people, and they may have accounted for up to 30 percent of completed youth suicides annually (Poland & Lieberman, 2003).

In December 2001, Mark Anderson and his colleagues from the Division of Violence Prevention of the Centers for Disease Control reported the results of a five-year study of violent deaths that had occurred either on the campus of a public school, on the way to or from regular school sessions, or during official school-sponsored events. They found that 220 confirmed school-associated incidents involving violent death had occurred between July 1, 1994, and June 30, 1999, with a total of 253 victims who died in those incidents. While 18 of the 220 total incidents were the widely reported school shootings that involved multiple victims, 202 of the incidents resulted in single deaths.

Analyzing the details of the 220 total incidents, 172 were homicides, 30 were suicides, and 11 were homicide-suicides. The remaining seven death-related incidents were the result of legal interventions into school situations or accidental firearms discharges. Over half of all these incidents were preceded by warning signals such as notes, journal entries, or threats; in the cases of suicides, significantly more than half were signaled in advance. Homicide perpetrators were also likely to have expressed suicidal behaviors, thoughts, or actual suicide attempts before the incidents (Anderson, et al., 2001).

Legal Implications for Educators

Imposing liability on schools and school personnel for failing to warn of a student's threats to commit suicide would require a showing of negligence on the part of school personnel. Negligence is a tort that requires proof of four elements that the plaintiff must show: (1) that the defendant had a duty of care, (2) that the defendant breached that duty, (3) that the breach of duty caused the damage alleged, and (4) that quantifiable damage actually occurred. The sticking point in the law is establishing that school personnel had a duty of care to prevent harm to the student.

Although no educator would deny a moral responsibility to care for and protect students in the school setting, a legal duty of care is different from a moral or professional duty. Courts have held that the requisite duty of care necessary in a suit for negligence against state actors occurs in only two different situations: (1) where individuals are under the control, or in the custody, of the state, as in an orphanage or in a jail; or (2) where the state itself created the danger. Courts have been reluctant to decide that either situation applies in the public school setting. Although school attendance is compulsory under state laws, schools are not jails or orphanages, and school employees are not wholly responsible for the care of students, nor are they in total control of students' actions or well-being.

State legislatures could, of course, make reporting of suspected student suicides by school personnel mandatory, as they have done for reporting suspected child abuse. However, to date few states have adopted specific statutory language dealing with school employees' obligations with respect to suspected student suicides or confidential communications from students. That said, the American Counseling Association does acknowledge that school counselors have an ethical obligation to report to parents, school administrators, or other appropriate authorities their suspicions that a student intends to harm herself or someone else. However, an association study in 1999 revealed that only 38 percent of school counselors believed that they could identify a student at-risk for suicide (Milson, 2002).

The situation is even more complicated when a student confronted with warning signs of her imminent suicide denies her intentions. Nicole Eisel, a 13-year-old Sligo Middle School student from Montgomery County, Maryland, confided to several friends her intent to commit suicide in a Satanic murder-suicide pact. When friends alerted school counselors, two counselors questioned Nicole, who vigorously denied making the comments. Neither counselor notified school authorities or the girl's parents. After Nicole committed suicide, her father brought a lawsuit against the counselors and the school district, alleging negligence as a cause of his daughter's death. Eisel argued that, if school authorities had not neglected their duty to warn him of Nicole's intentions, he could have prevented her suicide. The court granted summary judgment to the school district, stating that "public policy" prohibited recognizing that either the counselors or school district had a duty to intervene.

When Nicole's father appealed the decision, the Maryland Court of Appeals focused not on duty but on the foreseeability of the student's committing suicide. The court quoted from the Maryland State Department of Education's 1987 Youth Suicide Prevention School initiative for Maryland public schools, in place at Nicole's school at the time of her death, but declined to find that the law creating the program imposed liability on school counselors for failing to intervene in student suicides. Instead, the court pointed to the law as evidence of "a community sense that there should be intervention" when a student's emotional states indicates suicidal ideation. Even if the possibility of Nicole's committing suicide was remote, the court said, the possible harm was so "total and irreversible" that school counselors had a duty to "use reasonable means to attempt to prevent a suicide" when they had notice of a student's suicidal intent.

The Court of Appeals sent the case back to the lower court to determine if the counselors had sufficient notice of intent in order to hold them liable for failing to notify Nicole's parents. In an unreported decision, the jury hearing the evidence decided they did not. (For a discussion of unreported decisions, please see the end of Chapter 1.) The court then relieved the counselors and the school district of liability for Nicole's suicide. However, the *Eisel* decision has been interpreted in many jurisdictions as imposing on school counselors the duty to use reasonable means to prevent student suicides, including warning parents.

Parents of suicide victims have also attempted to sue school districts based on liability under Section 1983 of the federal Civil Rights Act of 1871, alleging that school officials acting under color of state law violated their children's civil rights. Shawn Wyke was a 13-year-old in 1989 when he finally accomplished at home the suicide he had twice before attempted in school. Shawn's mother sued the Polk County School Board and school officials at McLaughlin Junior High School where Shawn had been a student, alleging both negligence and violation of Section 1983. Mrs. Wyke argued that school personnel were made aware of Shawn's first suicide attempt after he tried to hang himself in the school bathroom, but district officials had not notified her or Shawn's grandmother, had not obtained counseling for Shawn, and had not taken him into protective custody. In 1995, in an unreported decision, a U.S. District Court jury dismissed Wyke's Section 1983 claim, stating that the district had no constitutional duty to protect Shawn Wyke from himself, but awarded her $165,000 damages on her state law claim that the school board negligently failed to supervise her son (Bjorklun, 1996). Wyke then appealed the court's dismissal of her Section 1983 federal claim.

In 1997, the U.S. Court of Appeals for the Eleventh Circuit ruled that Mrs. Wyke's Section 1983 claim failed. Failure to train school personnel in reporting and handling recurring situations where students are endangered was not enough to sustain a federal claim of violation of her son's constitutional rights, the court stated. The school, standing in the place of a student's parents, has a duty to supervise students. When a student attempts suicide at school, and the school knows of the attempt, the school can be found negligent in failing to notify a parent or guardian. However, compulsory school attendance laws do not give rise to a school district's constitutional duty to affirmatively protect students. In other words, under a Section 1983 federal claim analysis, school districts are not liable for student suicides.

What about a student who cannot deny his suicidal thoughts because he wrote them down? And what about school liability if the student's thoughts were submitted to a teacher in English class as an ongoing journaling assignment? Parents who seek to hold school districts liable for their children's suicides have a heavy burden of proof. In the case of Jeff Brooks, a high school student who chronicled his suicidal ideation for the four months of a daily journal-writing assignment in English class, the Idaho Supreme Court ruled that a jury could consider whether the district had violated a state law, as in Wyke's case, and been negligent in not notifying Jeff's parents of his troubled writings. However, the dissenting judge strongly stated that expecting teachers untrained in medicine to recognize and diagnosis a potentially suicidal student would "require a duty beyond reason."

Liability for Threats Resulting in Violence

When students carry out their threats in schools, and other students get hurt, are school districts or school personnel liable for the injuries to other students? Suppose the school district had warning signs of the dangers, teachers heard the threats or saw students acting out in unmistakably threatening ways?

Following the Columbine High School tragedy on April 20, 1999, many parents of injured and slain students sought to hold the Jefferson County School District, school officials, and law enforcement officials who had responded to the tragedy liable for injuries to their children. In the media aftermath of the Columbine shootings, the parents had discovered many reasons to think that school and law enforcement officials should have anticipated trouble at the hands of Dylan Klebold and Eric Harris. In January 1998, Klebold and Harris were apprehended by sheriff's deputies for stealing tools from a van, adjudicated delinquent, and placed in a county juvenile offender diversion program. Harris again came to the attention of law enforcement officials for repeatedly threatening the life of Brooks Brown, a fellow Columbine student. Harris maintained a Web site in which he spoke of issuing death threats, using pipe bombs to kill numerous people, and making other bombs. Sometime before the actual shootings, Harris added an "information panel" to his Web site listing as his "Hobbies" "Preparing for the big April 20! You'll be sorry that day."

The assistant principal in charge of discipline allegedly knew that Klebold and Harris had talked about blowing up the school. He had suspended them for hacking into school computers and stealing locker combinations. Klebold's creative writing teacher had alerted his guidance counselor to a particularly vicious story he wrote in her class. In his video production class, Harris turned in a videotape filmed inside the school depicting him and Klebold enacting revenge shootings of other Columbine students. Other videos showed the two shooters carrying guns in the school hallways and recorded their conversations about owning guns and making bombs. Their psychology teacher had heard them speak of their hatred, anger, and intent to kill other Columbine students in many classes.

The parents of Richard Castaldo, a student injured in the Columbine shootings, presented this evidence of the pre-April 20 warnings in a lawsuit alleging that both law enforcement and school officials had breached a duty of care to their son and violated his constitutional rights to be free from bodily harm by not taking steps to prevent the Columbine tragedy. The federal district court in Colorado dismissed their claims, stating that even if they were negligent, both law enforcement and school officials had such high social utility that to impose a duty on them to act affirmatively to prevent violent acts would undermine their usefulness to society as a whole. Affirming the general rule that compulsory attendance laws do not impose on schools an affirmative constitutional duty to protect students from harms imposed by others at school, the court rejected Castaldo's Section 1983 claim.

Months after the shootings, additional evidence came to light in the form of a journal written by Eric Harris and reports by the Brown family, and several other parents of injured students sued as the Castaldos had; all suits were dismissed from court. The Castaldos moved for reconsideration, but the court denied their request. One injured student attempted to sue the gun shop dealer who had sold guns to Klebold and Harris; his suit, too, was dismissed for the same reasons already stated.

Although the Colorado courts' assessment of the social utility of law enforcement and school officials is reassuring, the parents of slain and injured students in the Columbine community deserve some explanation of how and why professionals trained to deal with public school students ignored the collective signs of impending violence. As recently as October 2003, more information about forewarnings of the Columbine events was released by the current Jefferson County sheriff, Ted Mink, indicating that a caller had tipped authorities off to a threatening Web site created by Eric Harris as early as 1997 (Slevin, 2003). Threats and warning signs of violence have been present in other school shootings besides those at Columbine.

Courts may deny a school district's legal responsibility to act on threats and warnings of violence, even where the warning signs seem unmistakably clear in hindsight. However, school officials and school districts function at public expense. If courts were to impose liability on schools when students injure other students or teachers, even if warning signs were present and neglected, monetary damage awards might seriously deplete the public treasury, with benefits distributed to a relatively few individuals at the expense of the greater community. The same public policy argument applies in lawsuits against state-supported first responders in school shooting tragedies. Several states, including Idaho, where Jeffrey Brooks committed suicide, explicitly provide governmental entities immunity from lawsuits alleging liability for failure to adopt discretionary policies like suicide prevention programs. However, even Idaho has a statute requiring school boards to protect the health of its students. Florida, as the *Wyke* case demonstrates, has a law requiring school districts to immediately notify parents of any emergency involving students that occurs during the school day. The *Eisel* decision noted the Maryland statute mandating school districts' adoption of suicide prevention programs. Ohio has a similar suicide prevention initiative. One difficulty in assessing the prospects of school district liability for harms to students is the wide range of language used in state statutes dealing with student safety. Every statute seems to use different vocabulary terms, and courts hearing the lawsuits brought by the families of students injured or killed in schools are faced with interpreting the different terms on their own. Seemingly conflicting rulings may be the result. In addition, the law is distinctly different from morality and moral responsibility. The courts may legally set aside school districts' responsibility, but educators' moral responsibility is not so easily set aside.

The Take-Home Message on Threats

The legal standards for deciding what constitutes a true threat are confusing and contradictory. Until the Supreme Court steps in and defines a common standard test for all courts in the land to follow, the confusion and contradictory lower court opinions will persist. Unfortunately, the Supreme Court seems reluctant to undertake the needed clarification, and it has ignored several opportunities to deal with the issue.

What can and should educators do in the meantime? School personnel must take all threats or suspected threats seriously. Investigators have documented that many of the widely publicized recent episodes of school violence, such as those at Jonesboro and Columbine, were preceded by warnings or threats by the student perpetrators. Warning signs of student suicide may be subtle, but they are documented. All school personnel should be trained to recognize them. Warning signs include making verbal statements of a wish to die or an intent to commit suicide, cutting oneself or other intentional superficial self-wounding, experiencing prolonged depression, withdrawing, talking of death, putting affairs in order or giving away favorite possessions, or having a sudden change of mood to a kind of euphoria or extreme calm after a period of prolonged depression or anxiety.

For threats against the school community, the 1999 report of the Federal Bureau of Investigation's Critical Incident Response Group, *The School Shooter: A Threat Assessment Perspective*, recommends that schools adopt three-tiered threat response policies based on the perceived level of the threats: low level, carrying a minimal risk to the victim; medium level, threats that could possibly be effected but are not realistic; and high level, which pose a serious and imminent danger to others. *The Final Report and Findings of the Safe Schools Initiative: Implications for the Prevention of Attacks in the United States* (Vossekuil et al., 2002), issued by the U.S. Department of Education and the U.S. Secret Service, contains information about profiling students who make threats and sorting them into six categories. Another publication of the Department of Education and Secret Service, *Threat Assessment in Schools: A Guide to Managing Threatening Situations and to Creating Safe School Climates* (Fein et al., 2002), contains similar information. Both reports stress that "school shootings are rarely impulsive acts." The shooters told others, not the victims, but the other students did not tell adults.

The guiding principle in dealing with student threats should be that the first and foremost goal and duty of all school personnel is to safeguard the physical welfare of students and colleagues. Any and all threatening communications or materials should be reported to a school official with authority to investigate. The school official who receives such notification must research the reported incident and take appropriate action.

Of course, in an actual or perceived situation of a threatening nature, having policies in place to deal with the issue is always desirable, but the policies must be flexible enough to cover varied and possibly unanticipated circumstances. A useful exercise is to examine the scenarios described in this chapter and to determine whether the district has in place a student code of conduct or a district policy to deal with similar threatening situations. (All district policies should be incorporated in the student code of conduct by reference, and vice versa.) If not, codes and policies need to be put in place as soon as possible.

With appropriate documentation in place, the first step when a threat is made or suspected is to consult the district's student code of conduct to see whether the code itself or a district policy has been violated. If a part of the code or a policy has been violated, the designated consequence should be applied if the consequence is sufficient to deal with the severity of the issue. Any student who presents an immediate danger to school personnel or students should be removed from the school, with the assistance of school safety officers or the police if necessary, without any hesitation over possible legal action that may follow.

If the situation is deemed serious, district legal counsel should be involved as soon as possible. Courts will ultimately decide whether school personnel acted in accordance with the law, but an adverse decision years down the line is better than risking harm because of inaction when faced with the possibility of bodily harm to a member of the school community.

Annotated References and Resources

Constitutional and Statutory References

• The federal statute that makes it a crime to willfully and knowingly threaten the President of the United States is 18 U.S.C. § 871 (a).

• 18 U.S.C. § 875 (c) prohibits interstate communications containing threats to kidnap or injure another person, stating:

> Whoever transmits in interstate or foreign commerce any com-
> munication containing any threat to kidnap any person or any
> threat to injure the person of another, shall be fined under this
> title or imprisoned not more than five years, or both.

Many states also have state laws dealing with threatening communications. For example, California criminalizes making threats. To
prove that a defendant uttered a true threat, California Penal Code
§ 422 requires that the prosecution establish

> (1) that the defendant willfully threatened to commit a crime
> which will result in death or great bodily injury to another per-
> son, (2) that the defendant made the threat with the specific
> intent that the statement be taken as a threat, even if there is
> no intent of actually carrying it out, (3) that the threat—which
> may be made verbally, in writing, or by means of an electronic
> communication device—was on its face and under the cir-
> cumstances so unequivocal, unconditional, immediate and
> specific as to convey to the person threatened, a gravity of pur-
> pose and an immediate prospect of execution of the threat,
> (4) that the threat actually caused the person threatened to be
> in sustained fear for his or her own safety or for his or her
> immediate family's safety, and (5) that the threatened person's
> fear was reasonable under the circumstances.

Court Decisions
• The seminal Supreme Court decision on true threats is *Watts
v. United States*, 394 U.S. 705 (1969).

Student Threats of Harm to Others
• Sarah Lovell's case is *Lovell v. Poway Unified School District*, 90
F.3d 367 (9th Cir. 1996).

• In the University of Michigan e-mail case, "Jake Baker" was a pseudonym used by Abraham Jacob Alkabaz. His case is *United States v. Baker*, 890 F. Supp. 1375 (E.D. Mich. 1995), *aff'd United States v. Alkabaz*, 104 F.3d 1492 (6th Cir. 1997), *rehearing and suggestion for rehearing en banc denied* (1997).

• The two student rapper cases are *Doe v. Pulaski County Special School District*, 306 F.3d 616 (8th Cir. 2002) and *Jones v. Arkansas*, 64 S.W.3d 728 (Ark. 2002).

• Julius's real name is George, and his case is *In re George T.*, 102 Cal. App. 4th 1422 (Cal. Ct. App. 2002). Ryan D.'s case is *In re Ryan D.*, 100 Cal. App. 4th 854 (Cal. Ct. App. 2002).

• The creative writer is Douglas D., *In the Interest of Douglas D.*, 626 N.W.2d 725 (Wis. 2001).

• The student caught writing a bomb threat is Jason W., *In re Jason W.*, 837 A.2d 168 (Md. 2003).

School Districts' Duty to Report Student Threats of Suicide

• The *Tarasoff* duty is derived from *Tarasoff v. Regents of the University of California*, 551 P.2d 334 (Cal. 1976).

• Several courts have declined to recognize a school district's duty of care in suits for negligence. See, *J.O. v. Alton Community Unit School District 11*, 909 F.2d 267 (7th Cir. 1990); *D.R. v. Middle Bucks Area Vocational Technical School*, 972 F.2d 1364 (3d Cir. 1992).

• Lawsuits alleging district liability for student suicides include the following:

– *Eisel v. Board of Education of Montgomery County*, 597 A.2d 447 (Md. 1991), brought by Nicole Eisel's father.

– *Wyke v. Polk County School Board*, 898 F. Supp. 852 (M.D. Fla. 1995), and *Wyke v. Polk County School Board*, 129 F.3d 560 (11th Cir. 1997), both brought by Shawn Wyke's mother.

– *Brooks v. Logan*, 903 P.2d 73 (Idaho 1995), brought by Jeff Brooks' parents.

• Lawsuits against school officials and law enforcement authorities in the wake of the Columbine tragedy include:

– *Castaldo v. Stone,* 192 F. Supp.2d 1124 (D. Colo. 2001), *recon-
sideration denied,* 191 F. Supp.2d 1196 (D. Colo. 2002);
– *Graves v. Stone,* 191 F. Supp.2d 1194 (D. Colo. 2002);
– *Kirklin v. Stone,* 191 F. Supp.2d 1198 (D. Colo. 2002);
– *Ireland v. Jefferson County Sheriff's Department,* 193 F. Supp.2d
1201 (D. Colo. 2002).

Journal Articles, Texts, and Commentaries

• The National Center for Injury Prevention and Control of the
Centers for Disease Control reports that more people in the United
States die from suicide than from homicide. In 2000, 1.7 times as
many people committed suicides as were killed in homicides.
Available at www.cdc.gov/ncipc/factsheets/suifacts.htm (accessed
May 2004).

• Poland, S., & Lieberman, R. (2003, May). Questions
and answers: Suicide intervention in the schools. *National
Association of School Psychologists Communique 31*(7). Available at
www.nasponline.org/publications/cq317suicideqa.html (accessed
May 2004).

• Snyder, H. N., & Swahn, M. H. (2004, March). Juvenile suicides, 1981–1998. *Youth Violence Research Bulletin.* Available at
www.ncjrs.org/html/ojjdp/196978/contents.html (accessed May
2004).

• Department of Health and Human Services, Mental Health
(1999). *U.S. Department of Health and Human Services, Mental
Health: A Report of the Surgeon General.* Rockville, MD: Department
of Health and Human Services, National Institutes of Health, and
National Institutes of Mental Health. The Executive Summary is
available at http://www.surgeongeneral.gov/library/mentalhealth/
summary.html (accessed May 2004). Of particular interest is Chap-

ter 3, Depression and Suicide in Children, by Chavez, N., Hyman, S. E., and Arons, B. S. Available at www.surgeongeneral.gov/library /mentalhealth/chapter3/sec5.html (accessed May 2004).

• Anderson, M., et al. (2001, December 5). School-associated violent deaths in the United States, 1994–1999. *The Journal of the American Medical Association, 286*(21), 2695. Available at www.cdc.gov/ncipc/abstract.htm (accessed May 2004).

• Milson, A. (2002, March). Suicide prevention in schools: Court cases and implications for principals. *National Association of Secondary School Principals Bulletin, 86*(630). Available at www. principals.org/news/bltn_suicide0302.cfm (accessed May 2004).

• Court decisions involving student suicides are discussed in Bjorklun, E. C. (1996). School liability for student suicide. *Education Law Reporter, 106*(21).

• Slevin, C. (2003, October 30). Columbine pair stirred alarms as early as '97. *Philadelphia Inquirer*, p. A3. See also, Nussbaum, P. (2004, April 18). *Philadelphia Inquirer*, p. A1.

• O'Toole, M. E., & Critical Incident Response Group. (1999). *The school shooter: A threat assessment perspective.* Quantico, VA: National Center for the Analysis of Violent Crime. Available at www.fbi.gov/publications.htm (accessed May 2004).

• Vossekuil, B., Fein, R. A., Reddy, M., Borum, R., & Modzeleski, W. (2002). *The final report and findings of the safe schools initiative: Implications for the prevention of school attacks in the United States.* Washington, DC: U.S. Secret Service and U.S. Department of Education. Available at www.secretservice.gov/ntac_ssi. shtml (accessed May 2004).

• Fein, R., Vossekuil, B., Pollack, W., Borum, R., Modzeleski, W., & Reddy, M. (2002). *Threat assessment in schools: A guide to managing threatening situations and to creating safe school climates.* Washington, DC: U.S. Secret Service and U.S. Department of Education. Available at www.secretservice.gov/ntac_ssi.shtml (accessed May 2004).

CHAPTER SEVEN

Internet-Enabled Bullying, Harassment, and Threats

REMOTE, INSTANTANEOUS, AND ANONYMOUS, INTERNET-ENABLED COMmunication is the perfect vehicle for an insecure bully with instant-gratification urges. Bang out the message, pick a target, and shoot it on its way. Even the slang of its delivery mode gratifies with double entendre. Harassing messages are also easy to send—"Control-c, Control-v," with no need to even compose a new message every time. Innuendos and lies can be posted in chat rooms; blogs can ramble on, exposing personal angst and envy. Entire Web sites can be created in the privacy of a student bedroom and uploaded to the Web to bully, harass, and threaten fellow students, students in faraway schools, and school personnel anywhere.

The Internet in Schools

No doubt exists that the Internet has been both a boon and a burden to public schools. The Internet puts more information at students' fingertips than the old-fashioned *Encyclopædia Britannica* salesman could ever have carried. In fact, the entire encyclopedia, and many other comparable resources, is now available online, as are fully annotated reports, term papers, dissertations, and op-ed pieces on every conceivable subject. Students can use the Internet to do classroom-directed research, independent research, recreational research, or simply to play games.

The National Center for Educational Statistics (NCES) has charted the explosive expansion of the Internet into public schools and public school classrooms. Today, virtually all U.S. public schools have Internet access. Millions of federal tax dollars support the "e-rate" discount program for schools, enabling schools in even the poorest districts to purchase and support Internet-capable computers. In 1994, however, only 3 percent of instructional classrooms had Internet access; the care of the Internet was overwhelmingly consigned to school librarians. By 2002, according to the NCES, 87 percent of instructional classrooms had Internet access. That percentage increases daily. In 2002, the ratio of students to computers with Internet access in schools was 5:1, compared with 12:1 in 1998. NCES also reported that 75 percent of public schools had a Web site at the end of 2001 (NCES, 2002). Many districts now require individual teachers to maintain Web sites that parents can access for school and classroom news, student grades, and assignments.

The University of California at Los Angeles's *UCLA Internet Report: Year Three* (2003), a nationwide survey profiling attitudes and behaviors involved with Internet use, reports that 97 percent of all 12- to 18-year-olds use the Internet. Overall, Internet users spend 11 hours per week online, an increase of about 10 percent over the rate in 2002. The Internet has even edged out television; the UCLA survey found that as hours of Internet use increase, television viewing hours decrease. Streaming video presumably supplies the visual stimuli that today's generation craves.

Is the Internet making kids "smarter"? The jury seems to be out on that question, but the Internet is certainly providing students with tools that are more familiar and second nature to them than they are to many adults. The need for educators to be technologically savvy and confident Internet clients has become a given. The

International Society for Technology in Education (ISTE), a nonprofit professional organization with worldwide membership, has promulgated a tripartite set of standards for students, teachers, and administrators that specifically defines competencies that demonstrate technological literacy. The National Standards for Technology in Teacher Preparation and the National Educational Technology Standards for Administrators (NETS-A) are beginning to influence preservice teacher education curricula across the nation, as well as screening procedures for teacher and administrative candidates for public school positions. Many state standards documents incorporate required technology competencies for students.

As amazing as the Internet is as a source of scholarly information, it continues to present challenges for schools. Foremost is the matter of educating student Internet users to critically assess the sources of posted information. The virtual printed word on a computer screen is no more and no less reliable than its hard copy counterparts—books, magazines, and newspapers. Readers must critically assess the bias, background, and expertise of the information source and the reliability of the reporter.

Vying for primacy of importance is the challenge of educating students that just because an author or commentator uploads material to the Internet does not mean that the person is giving readers permission to copy the material freely. International and U.S. copyright laws protect Internet material with the same force as hard copy materials. Many educators and students do not realize that copyright notice is no longer required on copyrighted materials, or that they must treat all Internet materials as copyright protected unless the material in question explicitly states that it is freely copyable (Conn, 2002).

Issues of student and family privacy also arise in the school Internet context. Schools and school districts need to monitor carefully what they post on the Web as official school information and information from the central office, but they must also carefully monitor what each teacher, affiliated group, "Booster" club, parent organization, or sports team posts. District officials need to review the Family Educational Rights and Privacy Act (FERPA) to avoid disclosing personally identifiable student information on the Web without parental permission in violation of FERPA.

The Ugly Internet

Verifying authenticity of information, copyright concerns, and student privacy issues are all challenges exacerbated by Internet access in schools. However, these legal issues pale when compared with the student speech issues posed by the Internet and the possibilities that the Internet creates for bullying, harassment, and threats that can wreak havoc for both students and school personnel at the building and district levels.

The legal community has responded to student Internet speech issues on several levels. First Amendment advocates and various scholarly institutes have championed the rights of students to express their opinions freely on Web sites and in chat rooms and blogs. The courts have often upheld students' constitutional rights to unfettered Internet expression and reversed school disciplinary actions, sometimes even ordering districts to pay monetary damages or attorneys' fees to students and their families. Courts have also begun to scrutinize school district policies regulating student speech and districts' Internet acceptable-use polices. However, on the whole, courts more often defer to the expertise of school officials, applying jurisprudence developed in the trilogy of pre-Internet student speech cases—*Tinker v. Des Moines Independent School District*, *Bethel School District No. 403 v. Fraser*, and *Hazelwood School District v. Kuhlmeier*—to support school district decisions. On relatively rare occasions, courts have meted out criminal penalties for students whose Internet speech they judged to be criminally harassing or threatening.

One of the most telling determinatives of court outcomes in student Internet speech cases is how carefully and deliberately the teachers, building administrators, and district officials react when confronted with a potentially disruptive or damaging student expression situation. Courts severely admonish administrators whose knee-jerk reaction is to suppress student speech because they "don't like it." Teachers and administrators need to step back and consider the educational implications of *any* offensive or potentially harmful student expression, but especially in the Internet context, where the communication may have originated outside the school. Before taking action, they must consider and carefully enunciate the educationally defensible rationale for their planned response. If they do, and if they apply both legally and educationally defensible district policies in dealing with the situation, courts will more likely than not uphold their actions. The legal record is replete with examples of both good and bad outcomes for districts that all educators should consider.

Early Decisions on Students' School Internet Speech

Public school students began promulgating immature insults directed at teachers and school officials via the Internet almost as soon as they learned to master Web site construction. Sometimes they even managed to secure help from computer-savvy parents. The American Civil Liberties Union (ACLU) jumped into the legal fray to defend these early entrepreneurs of unsophisticated rudeness, and it obtained reversals of school-district disciplinary actions against the students.

Many of the early Internet expression lawsuits involved middle and high school students, typically male, who posted inappropriate, insulting, or lewd comments about teachers who had somehow irritated or angered them. Were these students trying to intimidate the teachers? Were they harassing the teachers? Or were they just "blowing off steam," saying online what they would have mumbled under their breath in the school hallways or with their friends in the cafeteria? Were they "retaliating" in a juvenile way for the perceived prejudiced or disagreeable treatment they received at the teacher's hands?

A Student with a Record of Problems

Take the example of Brandon Beussink. A high school junior at Woodland R-IV School District in Missouri in 1997–1998, Brandon created a Web page highly critical of his school administration, expressing his low opinion of the teachers, the principal, and the home page of the school in crude and vulgar language. He invited readers to express their own opinions about the issues by contacting the school principal and included a hyperlink from his Web page to the school's home page. Woodland's principal, Yancy Poorman, demonstrated a classic administrative knee-jerk response on viewing Brandon's critical remarks. Poorman decided on the spot "that there would be some discipline taken," and before the school day was out, he suspended Brandon from school for 10 days because he was "upset" that Brandon's demeaning message had been displayed on a school computer. Poorman did not stop to ascertain whether the student's Web site had caused any disturbance at school or even how frequently or widely accessed it had been at school.

When Brandon and his parents sued the school district, the district could not show that Brandon had ever intended that his Web site be accessed at school at all. Brandon's former girlfriend, acting on her own, accessed the Web page at school and showed it to her computer teacher because, she testified, she wanted to retaliate against Brandon after he had broken up with her. Applying the

Tinker standard, and finding no reasonable fear that Brandon's Web site rantings would interfere with school discipline, the U.S. District Court for the Eastern District of Missouri prevented the district from using Brandon's suspension to negatively affect his junior year grades. The court admonished the district, instructing that the public interest is served by allowing Brandon's "message" to be free from censure, thereby showing his peers the "protections of the U.S. Constitution and the Bill of Rights at work."

As appealing as the court's rhetoric was, even the most libertarian educators may find one aspect of Brandon's case disturbing. The court took note of Brandon's "unrelated improper conduct" at Woodland. School officials had previously disciplined the teenager for inappropriate use of school computers, and on one occasion he had been "violent and disrespectful" to the school librarian and banned from using the library computers as a result.

Was Brandon Beussink just blowing off steam, bringing matters of public concern to light and advocating community involvement? Or was he a volatile and potentially dangerous teenager whose previous violence and disrespectfulness at school merited psychological rather than disciplinary and judicial intervention? Was he harassing school officials in retaliation for being banned from the library computers? What does it mean when a student pens a crude and vulgar polemic directed at school personnel and shouts it to the world on the soapbox of the Internet? Keep in mind that the Missouri district court decided Beussink's case four months before the Columbine tragedy; perhaps the court would have decided his case differently after Columbine.

A Model Student

Unlike Brandon Beussink, Nick Emmett, a senior at Kentlake High School in Washington's Kent School District No. 415, was an outstanding student with a 3.95 GPA, a co-captain of the basketball team, and a generally no-nonsense student. On February 13, 2000, he posted obituaries of several students on a Web page that, like Brandon Beussink, he had created at home. The school principal placed him on "emergency expulsion" for, among other charges, intimidation, harassment, and disruption of the educational process at the school. The expulsion was subsequently modified to a five-day suspension and a prohibition against participation in school sports.

The U.S. District Court for the Western District at Seattle noted that school officials are "in an acutely difficult position after recent school shootings in Colorado, Oregon, and other places." Web sites, they continued, can be early warnings of a student's violent intentions. Nevertheless, the court decided that Nick was not one of those potentially violent students and prohibited the district from disciplining him. The ACLU ultimately brokered a settlement between Nick and the Kent School District in which the district agreed to pay Nick's attorneys' fees.

Other courts in different parts of the country decided similar cases, sometimes ruling for the student, sometimes for the district. Often educators felt that judges—working among adults and largely insulated from the surging hormones and developmental need to challenge authority that often govern middle and high school students—were insensitive to the feelings of vulnerability and defenselessness experienced by school personnel vilified on student Web sites. Judges, many educators believed, were too quick to champion student rights to freedom of expression and too slow to acknowledge the intimidation and victimization that school personnel felt when they were the targets of students' Internet scorn.

Pennsylvania Courts Side with a School District

A series of decisions in Pennsylvania, however, demonstrated that courts would acknowledge educators' rights to be free from

Internet vilification if the situation warranted. The situation in the picturesque, largely middle-class community of Bethlehem, Pennsylvania, became ugly enough for the courts to come down firmly on the side of the Bethlehem Area School District. Justin Swidler, a middle school student in May 1998 when he first posted his school-related Web site, became the center of a prolonged battle that dragged through the court system of Pennsylvania for more than five years. Created at home to vent his frustration with embarrassing incidents at school, Justin's Web site opened with a disclaimer that teachers and administrators from his school should not "enter" because the site contained material that would upset them (*Rice-Maue, 2000*).

On his Web site "Fulmer Sux," Justin expressed his hatred of his algebra teacher, Kathleen Fulmer. She "can't teach," she "can't read," and she "can't add," he wrote. He uploaded her picture and had her image morph into Adolf Hitler. Another picture of Fulmer showed her with her head chopped off and blood spurting from her neck. Swidler titled one section of the Web site "Why Should She Die" and asked readers to "give me $20 to help pay for the hit man." Other pages of the site included profanity and other insults directed to both Fulmer and the school principal, A. Thomas Kartsotis.

Justin bragged to fellow students about the Web site and accessed it in school. Overall, the site was accessed more than 200 times before both Kartsotis and Fulmer viewed the site, and it was ultimately taken down. The site caused disturbance for both students and teachers. Many viewed it as a real threat; students visited guidance counselors to talk about their fears. Fulmer was unable to continue teaching at the school, and substitutes were needed to cover her classes. The local newspaper found out about the Web site and initiated coverage that made headlines for months. Justin was suspended and ultimately expelled in September 1998.

Justin's parents enrolled him in a private school in Colorado. Apparently, his parents failed to share the complete story behind Justin's out-of-state education, and the school recognized his unique Web talents by making him school webmaster. After the Columbine shootings, Laura Schlessinger, a syndicated radio talk show host, appealed to listeners to "find" the dangerous Pennsylvania student hiding in Colorado. The media circus gained momentum.

Student and Parents Sue

In July 1999, Justin Swidler and his parents filed suit in Northampton County Court, seeking to reverse the school's disciplinary action. They alleged violation of the boy's constitutional rights, especially his First Amendment right to freedom of expression. The court upheld the district's actions, stating that district officials had not violated Justin's freedom of expression because his expression, advocating violence against school staff and materially disruptive to school operations, was not constitutionally protected. Quoting the three U.S. Supreme Court school speech decisions— *Tinker v. Des Moines Independent School District, Bethel School District No. 403 v. Fraser,* and *Hazelwood School District v. Kuhlmeier*—the Northampton County Court similarly dismissed the Swidlers' claims of other constitutional violations. Moreover, the court referred to the Bethlehem Area School District's own definition of harassment in its code of conduct, affirming the district's determination that Justin's Web site constituted harassment meriting disciplinary action. Justin, the court concluded, had intended harm, and his own statements to peers that he could get into trouble for publishing the Web site supported his own consciousness of guilt.

The county court's decision was just the first of four court rulings vindicating the actions of the Bethlehem Area School District in expelling Justin Swidler. The case ultimately ended in the

Pennsylvania Supreme Court, where, on September 28, 2002, the court upheld Justin's expulsion and agreed that the school district had not violated his constitutional rights.

Kathleen Fulmer took a sabbatical leave for medical reasons the year after Justin's expulsion. She tried to return to teaching, but even a transfer to another school in the district could not stem the notoriety that surrounded her. She left teaching for good, testifying later that she feared for her safety and the safety of her husband and students.

The Teacher and Principal Ultimately Win Damages

After an eight-day trial, a jury in November 2000 awarded Kathleen Fulmer and her husband $500,000 in damages in a civil suit against the Swidlers. Declining to recognize her claim for defamation—the court said students are not competent to judge the professional skill of their teachers, and, therefore, their evaluations cannot defame—the jury decided that Justin's Web site had invaded Fulmer's privacy and that his parents were guilty of negligent supervision, a civil tort. One month later, Principal Kartsotis settled his lawsuit against the Swidlers for an undisclosed amount. In a move that smacked of justifiable chutzpah, Fulmer and her husband went back to court to demand and to receive an additional almost $50,000 in interest on their damages award.

Some First Amendment activists view the Swidler case not as a triumph for a school district's ability to demand respectful student expression, but only as judicial pandering to an overly sensitive female teacher. Fulmer should have been more thick-skinned, they say, and should have just ignored Justin's Web site. Perhaps. However, the most vocal student rights activists do not work in public schools. In 1998, with recent school shootings in several parts of the country, what teacher could ignore the sight of her own image decapitated and bloody on a student-created Web site? After

Columbine, with the widely publicized link between students' Internet obsession and school violence, would any public school educator criticize Fulmer's reaction to reading a solicitation for money to hire a hit man to get rid of her?

As outrageous as the Swidler case was, it may be but the visible tip of the iceberg that the Internet may become for teachers and administrators. With districts releasing e-mail addresses of teachers and administrators to students, parents, and community members and requiring educators to post responses within certain limited time periods, schools and districts may be exposing educators as targets for unwarranted harassment. Parents who demand constant progress updates for their students regardless of justifiable educational needs, parents who dislike certain teachers for valid or invalid reasons, or any unreasonable individuals with e-mail access may become thorns in the sides of educators trying to do their best in a landscape of ever-increasing demands on their time. Offensive Web sites are not the only weapons of online tormentors.

Cyberbullying

Teachers and school personnel are not alone in being targets for Internet insults or intimidation. "Cyberbullying," online bullying of fellow students, is fast becoming the school bullies' tool of choice. In an article in the *Washington Post*, Rachel Simmons (2003) indicts Internet bullying as "the latest, most vicious trend in children's social cruelty" (p. B01). As more and more teenagers make Internet chat rooms, bulletin boards, and instant messaging a central part of their everyday lives, cyberbullying has the potential to affect more and more schools and students. The magnitude of the problem is suggested by the finding that by the end of 2003, a Google search on the word *cyberbullying* alone located more than 4,100 individual Web sites devoted to reporting the phenomenon and explaining how to deal with it (including, for example, www. bullyingonline.org, www.cyberguards.com, www.cyberangels.org, www.getnetwise.org, and www.haltabuse.org).

Although the courts have not yet wrestled definitively with issues of cyberbullying, educators see the potential for silent harm to vulnerable students. Gossip, innuendo, and outright lies promulgated through student-created Web sites, e-mails, chat rooms, and student blogs or online journals can be hard to trace, can originate and percolate outside the school radar or control, and can devastate students' reputations and self-esteem. As more and more schools provide students with free e-mail accounts and open access "public" folders, the possibility for abuse and anonymous intimidation originating in the schools increases. However, like the vulgar Web sites directed toward teachers and other school personnel, cyberbullying can also originate outside the school.

Because cyberbullies do not have to confront their victims directly, they may feel emboldened and uninhibited, making their messages more vicious than they would be in a personal confrontation. In addition, the inability to see the victim's reaction may impel the bully to meaner or more frequent attacks. And with increased opportunity and need to go online, for social interaction, school research, or homework assignments, the victims find it harder to escape. Even changing schools does not work.

Internet bullying is hard to trace. Internet service providers are not routinely required to identify users of their services. Most have policies requiring users to avoid posting offensive material, but enforcement mechanisms are ineffective for merely unpleasant postings. Unless the messages are actual threats directed at an individual, bullies usually remain anonymous. The Web site schoolscandals.com, run by a Nevada-based group of investors operating under the name Western Applications, functioned for years as a forum for California students to post anonymous gossip and derogatory comments about their peers, identified easily by school. More than 30,000 subscribers posted messages about students in more than 100 schools. School administrators, parents, and the local media in the San Fernando Valley finally succeeded in shutting down the site in April 2003. Parents also shut down schoolrumors.com, a similar site operating from the Denver area (Simmons, 2002).

Flame Mail and Hate Mail

Flame mail, e-mails meant to enrage and provoke readers, and *hate mail*, outright expressions of hatred directed to minorities or disfavored groups, are variants of cyberbullying. The Federal Bureau of Investigation (FBI) forcefully pursues leads about hate crimes perpetrated via e-mail. It has successfully prosecuted individuals who sent threatening e-mails directed at ethnic minorities on college campuses. Perhaps the most notorious case was that of Richard Machado, a student at the University of California at Irvine, who sent 58 e-mails to Asian students on campus, blaming them for campus crime and threatening to "make it my life career" to hunt them down and kill them. In May 1998, Machado was sentenced to one year in jail, but he was released under supervision for time served in prison awaiting trial. Many more Internet "flamers," however, operate under the radar of the FBI, perpetuating racial animosity and ill will toward minorities.

The Simon Wiesenthal Center, an international Jewish human rights organization that monitors hate Web sites, reports an alarming increase in the use of the Internet as a tool for disseminating hate messages and terroristic threats. Their sixth annual report, *Digital Terrorism and Hate 2004*, tallies over 4,000 Web sites posted by terrorists and extremists such as al Qaeda, Hamas, neo-Nazis, skinheads, and other hate groups. Even more alarming, many of these sites contain online recruitment videos designed to attract young people to their causes. Educators need to be aware of these attempts to pervert the idealism of students in their care so they can counter signs of hate groups' influence on impressionable young minds.

Cyberstalking

Unlike the more amorphous cyberbullying, cyberstalking is well known in the legal community. *Cyberstalking* is repeated harassing or threatening behavior accomplished via online means. As with offline stalking, many cyberstalkers are motivated by a desire to control their victims. The Internet provides anonymity and immediacy that may make a timid stalker more aggressive. That same anonymity can greatly exacerbate a victim's anxiety. Sophisticated cyberstalkers can use software programs to send messages at regular or random intervals when they are not even physically present at a computer terminal. The Internet also provides access to private information about many potential victims with simple search engines that provide detailed personal information with only basic prompts such as a telephone number. In addition, as with offline stalking, cyberstalking can be a prelude to actual physical violence.

In a study of 470 cybercrimes investigated by the New York City Police Department's Computer Investigation and Technology Unit between January 1996 and August 2000, 42.8 percent (or 201) of the cases involved aggravated harassment by computer or Internet use. Of the 134 cases closed with a suspect arrested, offenders had used e-mail to harass their victims in 79 percent of the cases. Instant messages were used in 13 percent of the cases. Although the most likely targets of the harassers were women, educational institutions were the second most likely target. Approximately 26 percent of the perpetrators of the harassment were juveniles under the age of 16. One offender was only 10 years old! (D'Ovidio & Doyle, 2003)

Laws Against Cyberstalking

The attorney general of the United States, at the request of then–vice president Al Gore, issued the *1999 Report on Cyber-Stalking: A New Challenge for Law Enforcement and Industry.* The report notes the growing scope and complexity of the problem of cyberstalking and the need for both law enforcement and ISPs to crack down on cyberstalking. Law enforcement agencies in 2003 estimated that electronic communications are a factor in 20–40 percent of all stalking cases.

Several federal laws provide mechanisms to address cyberstalking, although do not prohibit the offense specifically. For example, federal law 18 U.S.C. § 875 (c) makes it a crime to transmit any communication in interstate or foreign commerce containing a threat to injure another person. However, although the Internet easily qualifies as an interstate communication, the requirement that an actual threat be communicated may make it difficult to reach cyberstalkers who merely harass or intimidate without explicit threats. Other federal laws explicitly prohibit harassment by electronic means, such as 47 U.S.C. § 223, but because that law requires a direct communication between stalker and victim, it would not cover a situation where a cyberstalker posts messages on a bulletin board or Web site or in a chat room. The Violence Against Women Act of 2000, signed into law by President William Clinton in October 2001, extends the federal stalking statute to include stalking by mail, telephone, or the Internet but also uses the legal term of art, *threat*, that could prove a deterrent to conviction for a cyberstalker.

Many states have attempted to fill the gaps in federal protection by passing their own state statutes prohibiting electronic stalking. The National Conference of State Legislatures (2003) reports that 45 states had laws that explicitly included electronic communication within stalking or harassment laws. North Carolina is the only state to date to adopt a statute specifically and exclusively directed at cyberstalking. At least one state, Louisiana, specifically criminalizes electronic stalking of children within its general stalking statute.

School Web Sites and Cyberstalking

Many law enforcement agencies have recognized the seriousness and widespread nature of cyberstalking and have established specialized units to investigate and deal with the problem. For example, the New York City Police Department established their Computer Investigation and Technology Unit, and Los Angeles developed a Stalking and Threat Assessment Team. These units train law enforcement officers to use "electronic trails" like conventional fingerprints to track cyberstalkers. However, cyberstalkers are not limited geographically to large metropolitan areas, and school Web sites can provide attractive and accessible information about potential victims. Schoolchildren are not immune to cyberstalking. They may also naively reveal sensitive personal information once a stalker makes contact or be easily seduced into a personal meeting that exposes them to physical harm. School district and school personnel need to be especially alert to the possibility of providing opportunities for pedophiles and cyberstalkers to initiate personal relationships with students of any age.

In 1995, the FBI launched a national undercover initiative, Innocent Images National Initiative, to expose and investigate suspected child pornography and sexual exploitation of children online. In addition to establishing an Internet presence as a deterrent to would-be pedophiles and child molesters, the initiative seeks to prosecute sexual predators and to rescue child victims. In its first three years of operation, Innocent Images resulted in 232 convictions. However, from 1996 to 2002, the FBI experienced an astounding 1,997 percent increase in the number of cases opened, from 113 to 2,370. No one can doubt the reality of the danger of exposing children's identities on the Web.

Cyberthreats

Cyberthreats can be hard to deal with both emotionally for victims and legally for law enforcement officials. The law will usually recognize a threat as credible or as a "true threat" only if delivered personally or directly to an individual. Bullies and stalkers, especially cyberbullies and cyberstalkers, often do not directly threaten their victims; they engage in a pattern of repeated behaviors that, taken in context, leads the victim to feel threatened. However, no specific words that constitute a threat of bodily harm may be actually communicated. For students, particularly teenage girls, an added burden may be the possibility of being dismissed as hysterically overreacting to simple unwanted attention.

A most egregious example of the inadequacy of laws dealing with cyberthreats is the Jake Baker case, discussed at length in Chapter 6. Baker, a University of Michigan student later identified as Abraham Jacob Alkabaz, shared with a Canadian chat room friend explicit fantasies of sexually molesting and torturing women and young girls. In his e-mails, Baker actually named a female university classmate as a woman he wanted to rape, mutilate, and murder. When law enforcement officials attempted to take legal action against him, Baker successfully avoided criminal prosecution by convincing the court that his graphic descriptions of rape and torture of his female classmate and other young women were not true threats. The case demonstrates how difficult it may be to prove that a cyberthreat is a true threat for which the perpetrator will be held accountable under the law.

Annotated References and Resources

Constitutional and Statutory References

• The Family Educational Rights and Privacy Act (FERPA), 20 U.S.C. § 1232 g, protects the confidentiality of students' education records and the rights of parents to access such records. More detailed information about FERPA is available at www.ed.gov/offices/OM/fpco/ferpa/index.html (accessed May 2004).

• 18 U.S.C. § 875 (c) prohibits interstate communications containing threats to kidnap or injure another person.

• 47 U.S.C. § 223 prohibits making obscene or harassing telecommunications in the District of Columbia or in interstate or foreign communications.

• The statute under which Richard Machado was criminally prosecuted is 18 U.S.C. § 245 (b) 2 (A), which prohibits interference with Federally Protected Activities (in this case, the rights of Asian students to education).

Court Decisions

• The three seminal student speech cases, decided by the U.S. Supreme Court in 1969–1988:

– *Tinker v. Des Moines Independent School District*, 393 U.S. 503 (1969).
– *Bethel School District No. 403 v. Fraser*, 478 U.S. 675 (1986).
– *Hazelwood School District v. Kuhlmeier*, 484 U.S. 260 (1988).

• The two student Web site decisions in which the courts ruled against the school districts:

– *Beussink v. Woodland R-IV School District,* 30 F. Supp.2d 1175 (E.D. Mo. 1998).
– *Emmett v. Kent Lake School District No. 415,* 92 F. Supp.2d 1088 (W.D. Wash. 2000).

• The four decisions in which the Pennsylvania courts upheld the right of the Bethlehem Area School District to discipline Justin Swidler were *J.S. v. Bethlehem Area School District* at

– 51 Northampton County Reporter 181, 182 (Northampton County 1999),
– No. 1998-CE-5770 (Northampton County Court of Common Pleas 1999),
– 757 A.2d 412 (Pa. Commw. 2000), *reargument denied,* and
– 807 A.2d 847 (Pa. 2002) (the final decision of the Supreme Court of Pennsylvania).

• Richard Machado appealed his conviction under 18 U.S.C. § 245 (b) 2 (A) in *United States v. Machado,* 195 F.3d 454 (9th Cir. 1999), arguing a procedural violation that was denied by the Court of Appeals for the Ninth Circuit. No other legal citations for his case are available in national court reporters.
• The Jake Baker case, discussed at length in Chapter 6, is *United States v. Baker,* 890 F. Supp. 1375 (E.D. Mich. 1995), *aff'd United States v. Alkabaz,* 104 F.3d 1492 (6th Cir. 1997), *rehearing and suggestion for rehearing en banc denied* (1997).

Journal Articles, Texts, and Commentaries

• NCES (2002). *Internet access in U.S. public schools and classrooms: 1994-2002.* Available at http://nces.ed.gov/surveys/frss/

publications/2004011/ (accessed May 2004). NCES (National Center for Education Statistics) is the primary federal entity for collecting and analyzing education-related data for the United States and other countries.

• Lebo, H. (2003, February). *UCLA Internet report: Year three.* Los Angeles: The University of California at Los Angeles (UCLA) Center for Communication Policy. The study is the third in a series of annual nationwide surveys investigating behaviors and attitudes about Internet use and impact on society. The report is available at http://ccp.ucla.edu (accessed May 2004).

• The International Society for Technology Education (ISTE) is the professional organization responsible for developing and promulgating the National Educational Technology Standards for students, teachers, and administrators. The overall goal of the standards is to help students "live, learn, and work successfully in an ever-increasingly complex and information-rich society," according to the mission statement of ISTE at its Web site, www.iste.org. The foundation standards for teachers set out performance indicators describing effective technology use by teachers. NETS-A is the corresponding set of performance indicators for administrators. All standards are available at http://cnets.iste.org. ISTE has also developed performance standards for teacher accreditation programs in educational computing and technology through its National Council for Accreditation of Teacher Education (NCATE). The NCATE standards are available at multiple hyperlinks on the ISTE Web site.

• Conn, K. (2002). *The Internet and the law: What educators need to know.* Alexandria, VA: Association for Supervision and Curriculum Development.

• Rice-Maue, L. (2000, October 31). Boy's father testifies about vulgar Web site: Howard Swidler says it 'was quite inappropriate. I was very unhappy with what he had done.' *Morning Call,* p. B03.

The online archives of *The Morning Call* detail aspects of Justin Swidler's legal battle against the Bethlehem Area School District, which dominated several courts in Pennsylvania for months. The articles are available for a fee at www.mcall.com (accessed May 2004).

• Simmons, R. (2003, September 28). Cliques, clicks, bullies and blogs. *Washington Post*, p. B01. The article is available for a fee at www.washingtonpost.com (accessed May 2004).

• The schoolscandals.com shutdown by concerned parents in the San Fernando Valley, California, was reported in

– Associated Press. (2003, March 25). 'Cyberbullying' Web site in California shut down. *USA Today.* Available at http://usatoday.com/tech/webguide/internetlife/2003-04-25-cyber bullying_x.htm (accessed May 2004).

– *eSchool News* (2003, June 1). School gossip site folds following complaints from kids and angry parents. Available with registration at www.eschoolnews.com/news/issue.cfm?Pub ID=1& IssueID=197.

• The shutdown of schoolrumors.com by parents was reported in the following:

– Simmons, R. (2002, May 6). Bullying, girl-style: They roll their eyes, gossip maliciously and turn on friends. *Los Angeles Times.* Also available at www.rachelsimmons.com (accessed May 2004).

– Welch, M. (2001, March 12). Off-campus speech v. school safety. *Online Journalism Review.* Available http://ojr.org/ojr/ ethics/1017961581.php (accessed May 2004).

- The report *Digital Terrorism and Hate 2004* is available as a CD-ROM at the Web site of the Simon Wiesenthal Center at www.wiesenthal.com/social/press/pr_item.cfm?ItemID=9277 (accessed May 2004).
- The New York City Police Department Computer Investigation and Technology Unit (CITU) is described by D'Ovidio, R. and Doyle, J. (2003, March). A study on cyberstalking: Understanding investigative hurdles. *FBI Law Enforcement Bulletin, 72*(3), p. 10, Available at http://articles.findarticles.com/p/articles/ mi_m2 194/is_3_72/ai_99696472 (accessed May 2004).
- 1999 Attorney General of the United States' Report on Cyber-Stalking: A New Challenge for Law Enforcement and Industry is available at www.usdoj.gov/criminal/cybercrime/cyberstalking.htm (accessed April 2004).
- The Los Angeles Stalking and Threat Assessment Team is described at http://da.co.la.ca.us/stalking.htm (accessed May 2004).
- The Innocent Images National Initiative is described at ww.fbi.gov/hq/cid/cac/innocent.htm (accessed May 2004).

CHAPTER EIGHT

Recommendations and Plans for Action

WITH FUNDING PROVIDED UNDER THE SAFE AND DRUG FREE SCHOOLS and Communities Act of 1994, over 70 percent of the largest school districts in the country have installed metal detectors in their schools. With the passage of the Gun Free Schools Act, also in 1994, Congress gave schools the go-ahead to establish "zero toler-ance" policies and provided federal funding to expel students who bring weapons to school and turn the students over to juvenile authorities.

Metal detectors and zero tolerance policies may have con-tributed to the dramatic reduction in the number of violent crime victims in schools from 1992 to 2000, a decrease of 46 percent, according to the National Center for Educational Statistics (2002); but they have not been shown to decrease bullying, harassment, or threats that do not result in reported physical injury. On the con-trary, according to all commentators in the field, bullying is on the rise in public schools, harassment is alive and well, and threats and threatening behaviors persist.

Zero Tolerance

A *zero tolerance policy* is a school or district policy that mandates predetermined consequences, discipline, or punishments for certain identified offenses (e.g., carrying a weapon to school). It began as the name of a 1986 governmental program that impounded boats carrying drugs. The Gun Free Schools Act gave the policy a resurgence in education, requiring school districts that accept federal funds to adopt gun-free school policies and to expel for a year students who carry guns to school. Although schools may modify the expulsion policy on a case-by-case basis, the act spurred the adoption of inflexible zero tolerance policies.

Frank G. Green, the executive director of Keys to Safer Schools (1999), charges that zero tolerance policies simply do not work. He relates stories of zero tolerance gone wrong: the teen whose father was serving in the military, suspended because he drew a stick figure of a U.S. Marine shooting a man; another student suspended because he wrote a Hollywood-style horror story. Other critics of zero tolerance are supporting the legal action of Christina Hyun Lough, a Katy, Texas, junior high student disciplined after bringing to school a traditional Korean pencil sharpener purchased in Korea by her parents. School authorities imposed a seven-day in-school suspension and removed Christina from her post as president of the student council and honor society (*Houston Chronicle*, October 22, 2003; November 20, 2003).

While Christina's lawsuit is in its infancy, the lawsuit brought by the father of kindergarten student A.G., disciplined under his school's zero tolerance policy, is winding its way toward the U.S. Supreme Court. A.G., playing a game of "cops and robbers" with his friends at recess in the schoolyard of the Wilson Elementary School in Sayreville, New Jersey, yelled out, "I'm going to shoot you." Another student told a teacher, who took A.G. to the principal's office. The principal suspended the kindergartner for three days.

A.G.'s father, upset when notified of the suspension, contacted the district superintendent, who supported the principal's action, saying, "Policy is policy." A.G.'s father brought suit, alleging violation of his son's constitutional rights to free speech, due process, and equal protection of the laws. The district court granted summary judgment to the district, noting the school's concern with recent student threats and speech about guns. The father appealed.

The Third Circuit Court of Appeals, considering the free speech issue raised, looked to the three seminal student speech cases—*Tinker*, *Fraser*, and *Kuhlmeier*—and ruled that the school was within its rights when disciplining A.G. The school, the court said, must foster "socially appropriate behavior"; where concern existed about student threats and simulated gun use, disciplining A.G. for his speech about killing was proper. A.G. was not expressing a political opinion about gun use; his young age gave the school even more justification for regulating his expression. In any event, school officials were "acting within the scope of their permissible authority in deciding that the use of threatening language at school undermines the school's basic educational mission." The court explicitly affirmed the school's right to adopt a zero tolerance policy. Zero tolerance policies, according to the Third Circuit Court, do not violate students' due process rights.

A.G.'s father petitioned the U.S. Supreme Court to grant *certiorari* and hear his son's case. In January 2004 the Court refused. Such a refusal usually signals to legal scholars one of two things: either that the justices of the Supreme Court are substantially in agreement with the decision of the lower court, or that the justices do not feel that the time is right to resolve the issue. Both advocates and critics of zero tolerance are monitoring the accumulation of student lawsuits resulting from enforcement of zero tolerance policies with concern (Jenkins & Dayton, 2002).

The inflexibility of zero tolerance policies results in automatically imposed penalties in situations where administrators, if free to use their discretion, would likely have investigated and acted more in keeping with the reality of the situation. More and more students are being excluded from public education for relatively minor infractions. Even more noteworthy, however, is the criticism that zero tolerance policies discriminate against students of color, especially blacks. The Advancement Project and the Civil Rights Project (2000) joint study found that zero tolerance policies contributed to students of color frequently receiving harsher discipline than their white counterparts for similar offenses. Nationally, the study found, black students constitute 17 percent of the nation's public school children but 32 percent of all suspensions. On the other hand, no data indicate that zero tolerance policies are reducing bullying, harassment, or more serious threatening behaviors in public schools.

Antibullying Statutes

In September 2003, New Jersey became the latest state to pass legislation requiring school districts to adopt antibullying policies and to implement methods for responding to bullying and other forms of harassment. New Jersey's law requires that the new policies contain a statement prohibiting the bullying, harassment, or intimidation of a student; a definition of the offense and the consequences for committing the offense; a description of the behavior expected from students; and the procedures for reporting and investigating complaints. Districts must also enumerate the range of school responses upon notification of an offense. Randy Ross of the New Jersey Department of Law and Public Safety stressed the importance of early intervention in bullying situations to change the "culture of bullying" the department felt had developed in schools (Bitman, 2003).

All 50 states now have antibullying statutes, antiharassment statutes, or a combination of both. The problem is that each state's law is different; each deals with different aspects of the problem. Vermont's statute, for example, deals with bullying, harassment, and hazing. Some states have passed new laws in response to what lawmakers perceive as an increasing problem of bullying in schools. Other states have merely retrofit older laws prohibiting intimidation or threats to apply to bullying and harassment issues. Still others, like Pennsylvania, attempt to deal with bullying and harassment by mandating school districts' adoption of character education programs.

Many states have adopted "safe schools legislation" but have failed to incorporate enforcement mechanisms into the statutory language. Most statutes fail to provide for a private right of action that would enable parents and community members to take schools to task for not implementing the laws. Even Oregon's law, which provides for parent and community input into the development of school bullying policies, provides no process for enforcement. Oklahoma and Colorado have adopted similar legislation, also requiring parental and community involvement. Although the laws are steps in the right direction, they fall short of providing for ongoing review of the effectiveness of the statutes and policies adopted under their mandates.

One of the problems with antibullying programs is defining what constitutes bullying with sufficient precision. Take, for example, the "explanation" of bullying from the Virginia state antibullying statute. Virginia's statute prohibits harassment, intimidation, and bullying, which the statute defines collectively as "conduct that disrupts a student's ability to learn and a school's ability to educate its students in a safe, non-threatening environment." Further conflating the terms *bullying*, *harassment*, and *threats*, the statute continues by defining them as "any intentional gesture, or any intentional written, verbal or physical act or threat that . . . is sufficiently severe, persistent or pervasive that it creates an intimidating, threatening or abusive educational environment." Can any educator, after reading the explanation of conduct prohibited in Virginia, distinguish among the behaviors that characterize bullying, harassment, and threats in Virginia, or determine how to apply legal precedents adjudicating behaviors labeled as bullying, harassment, or true threats in U.S. courts? Simple teasing, if repeated often, may be an unlawful behavior in Virginia.

In U.S. jurisprudence, judges and legal scholars agonize over the nuances of words. In the law, bullying does not equal harassment, harassment is not the same as a threat, and verbal bullying may be an activity protected under the First and Fourteenth Amendments. True threats are never constitutionally protected. Precision in language is important in a court of law, and antibullying statutes that purport to ameliorate all woes perpetrated by one individual on another may be struck down in the courts as unconstitutionally overbroad or vague. In addition, they may be practically unhelpful in trying to educate students about appropriate and inappropriate behaviors, as well as degrees of inappropriateness among them. Antibullying statutes should prohibit bullying, and bullying should be carefully and uniquely defined in each statute. Children, at a developmentally appropriate age, should be taught that other behaviors, related to but potentially more serious than bullying, are also inappropriate. These would be sexual, racial, ethnic, disability-based, or age-related harassment or true threats of violence toward another.

Statutes Prohibiting Sexual or Gender Orientation Discrimination

Like states that mandate school district adoption of antibullying programs, several states also mandate school district adoption of antidiscrimination policies dealing with gender orientation. According to the National Center for Lesbian Rights, eight states and the District of Columbia prohibit discrimination or harassment in schools on the basis of sexual orientation. The eight states are

California, Connecticut, Massachusetts, Minnesota, New Jersey, Vermont, Washington, and Wisconsin. California, Minnesota, and New Jersey also explicitly prohibit discrimination or harassment in schools based on gender identity (Marksamer & Joslin, 2004). Sexual or gender orientation, having a preference for same sex relationships, is differentiated from gender identity, which has to do with expressing gender, as in dress, manner, or style (Human Rights Campaign Foundation, 2004).

Neither gender orientation nor sexual identity is protected under Title VII, the federal law that prohibits sexual harassment of students, but courts have ruled that gay, lesbian, and bisexual students or those perceived as such have the right to be free from discrimination under the Equal Protection clause of the Fourteenth Amendment. In fact, a recent court settlement between the Morgan Hill Unified School District near San Jose, California, and students who alleged that they had been discriminated against because of their gender orientation, cost the district $1.1 million. The district will also have to provide mandatory training for teachers, administrators, and other staff members to eliminate harassment and discrimination against gay and lesbian students. Finally, the district must establish antiharassment programs for 7th and 9th graders.

The settlement followed the refusal of the Court of Appeals for the Ninth Circuit to side with the school district in a lawsuit brought by a group of former students. The students alleged that they had been harassed in Morgan Hills schools for years because of their gender orientation, and that the district had been deliberately indifferent to their plight, despite antidiscrimination policies in place in the district. The students reported name-calling by other students, trash thrown at them, and insults scrawled on their lockers. Administrators took no action against the perpetrators. One student, while in middle school, was called "faggot" by classmates who beat him so severely that he required hospitalization. The school transferred him to another school; administrators punished only one student.

The Ninth Circuit ruled that a jury could find that the school district's refusal to enforce existing district polices prohibiting peer harassment to protect all students equally, without reference to gender orientation, violated the Equal Protection clause of the Fourteenth Amendment. The out-of-court settlement followed in January 2004, approximately nine months after the court's decision. Many school districts are looking at the settlement figure as a high priced warning signal.

Reporting Violence Under the No Child Left Behind Act

President George W. Bush's controversial No Child Left Behind (NCLB) law, passed in 2001, requires school districts to gather statistics on school violence and to report these statistics to the public on a school-by-school basis. Based on a Texas law that requires all schools to report incidents of violent activity, NCLB provides that states must define and identify "persistently dangerous schools." Schools so identified must offer students the chance to attend a different public school in the district. However, states differ in the definitions of persistently dangerous.

In the first year of required reporting (2003–2004), 44 states plus the District of Columbia reported no persistently dangerous schools. Only 54 schools out of the approximately 91,000 public schools in the country identified themselves as persistently dangerous under state defined criteria, and half of those schools were in the city of Philadelphia. Neither Detroit, Chicago, Miami, Los Angeles, nor neighboring Newark or Trenton, reported any persistently dangerous schools. Paul Vallas, superintendent of the Philadelphia Public Schools, characterized his Philadelphia schools as the "victims of our own aggressiveness" (Robelon, 2003). Clearly, Philadelphia is not the only city in the country where school violence is a problem.

In addition to the definitional and reporting issues, the NCLB "solution" puts the burden of remedying violence on the victim of the violence. It is the victim who must switch schools, leaving friends and neighborhood, incurring added travel time to and from school, while the perpetrator remains in familiar surroundings, perhaps to seek and find a new victim.

Devising Policies to Deal with Bullying, Harassment, and Threats

School or school district policies that address bullying, harassment of students, or student threats must be broad-based, because students who engage in these behaviors do not conform to any stereotype; they do not come from a predetermined background but from all kinds of homes and home situations. Collaboration with other community social organizations is important. School violence is a community, not a school-only, problem.

That said, school districts and all governmental agencies must keep in mind the tension between the guarantees of the First Amendment to freedom of speech and the duty of state actors to regulate student expression. Dealing with students' true threats of violence is substantively different from regulating students' bullying or harassing messages, and imposing penalties for harassing speech is different from punishing harassing conduct. Neither true threats of violence nor harassing conduct are protected by the First Amendment. Purely nasty speech may be.

The Third Circuit Court of Appeals made the State College Area School District in Pennsylvania keenly aware of the distinctions in its 2001 ruling on a lawsuit brought against the district by group of fundamentalist Christians who objected to the district's new speech policy. Intended to establish a "safe, secure, nurturing school environment" in the schools where disrespect was unacceptable, the policy prohibited harassment "based on race, religion, color, national origin, gender, sexual orientation, disability, or other personal characteristics." The Christian group objected to the policy because they said it prevented students from speaking out against homosexuality, which was their religious responsibility.

The court, more sympathetic to the dictates of the First Amendment than to the school district's desire for respectful speech, ruled that it was lawful for the school district to prohibit speech that discriminated on the basis of race, color, or national origin under Title VI; sex under Title IX; disability or age under the Rehabilitation Act; or harassment in the workplace under Title VII. However, the majority continued, where the policy prohibits disparaging speech based on personal values, it is unconstitutionally overbroad. Trying to keep students from insulting one another based on personal characteristics may be futile or just plain "silly," the majority continued, but prohibiting speech simply because it is offensive or unpleasant goes against America's "bedrock principle" of the First Amendment.

Whereas the *Saxe* decision is controlling authority only in the states of the Third Circuit, the reminder and warning is worth bearing in mind. Overbroad policies may be ruled unconstitutional if challenged in the courts. Similarly, policies may also be ruled unconstitutional if they are vague. The prohibited conduct must be stated explicitly, and students should be put on notice of the consequences for violations.

Any bullying, harassment, or student threat policies adopted by individual schools or school districts should carefully define what is covered under the policy. A separate policy, or separate sections of an inclusive policy, is recommended for each prohibited behavior, with consequences spelled out for each different offense and repeated violations of the same offense. The policy should establish a complaint procedure and name an individual who bears ultimate responsibility for summarizing the results of school or district investigations into allegations of inappropriate behaviors. The steps that will be followed in an investigation should be listed, although the list may state that the steps enumerated are not necessarily the only ones that may be necessary in a given investigation.

Provisions to protect victims and reporters from retaliation should be part of the policy, and rewards for informants may be included as incentives to break the code of silence that may surround activities that need investigating. The policies need to include provisions for training personnel in their implementation and mechanisms for dissemination of information about their provisions to students, school personnel, and community members at large. Training should be ongoing, and its schedule documented, so that new students, staff, and community members receive information in a timely fashion.

District counsel should be included, if possible, in training. If a lawsuit occurs as a result of a policy violation, a lawyer will be scrutinizing how the district investigated complaints. It is better to have a lawyer at both the beginning and the end of any story, especially a lawsuit.

If law enforcement officials need to be called in, districts need to put out the necessary call. However, waiting for the police officer is not an excuse to do nothing. School officials need to stop the prohibited behavior and begin their own independent investigation and documentation of the circumstances, with personal interviews, open-ended questions, written records, photographs, and any other durable evidence collections. The district superintendent should be advised of any and all actions taken.

Increased supervision of students has been identified as the key to preventing school violence. Many schools have tightened security and require all students and teachers to wear identification badges. Resource personnel monitor school entrances. School resource officers patrol hallways. However, impersonal monitoring efforts such as these may only seal the determination of disruptive students to avoid detection and, therefore, prove counterproductive in preventing inappropriate and unlawful conduct by students lawfully in attendance in the school. Increased student supervision must be truly student centered. Such supervision and personalized attention to individual students is difficult to accomplish in the megaschools that some districts favor or that population pressures mandate. However, teachers and administrators have little chance to find out about problems such as bullying, harassment, and threats without direct involvement and personal, caring interaction with students. Many schools have initiated after-school, or extended day, programs in which teachers can get to know students in a less formal setting. Student clubs as part of the school day accomplish the same goal.

Character Education Programs

Many antibullying and antiharassment programs adopted by schools are based on, or have strong ties with, traditional character development programs. Multicultural programs have also been introduced in schools to help combat racial harassment in the schools.

One of the most successful programs, the Olweus Bullying Prevention Program, first developed in Norway in response to widely publicized student suicides there, claims to achieve a 50 percent reduction in bullying and other antisocial behaviors in schools that implement the program (Olweus, Limber, & Mihelic, 1999). The Olweus program starts with a survey to determine the extent of bullying in the school. The program requires the appointment of an antibullying coordinator and mandates training for all administrators and teachers, as well as selected students and parents. School rules against bullying are established, and classes discuss bullying. Supervision is increased, and adults are encouraged to intervene affirmatively in suspect situations. Individual, personal interventions with known school bullies are initiated. The Center for the Study and Prevention of Violence based at the University of Colorado has qualified the Olweus Bullying Prevention Program as a model program in its Blueprints for Violence Prevention series.

Another character education program, Linking the Interests of Families and Teachers (LIFT), also claims significant, long-term results similar to those of the Olweus program (Fox, Elliot, Kerlikowske, Newman, & Christeson, 2003). Less well-known, and therefore less widely implemented, LIFT has been evaluated with both 1st and 5th grade students, with whom it proved effective in significantly reducing aggressive behaviors on school playgrounds. First graders who received LIFT interventions showed lower levels of inattentive, impulsive, and hyperactive behaviors when they reached 4th grade than did peers who had not received the interventions. Fifth graders in the study who had not received LIFT interventions were twice as likely to be arrested in middle school compared with peers who had received the interventions.

LIFT interventions include parental involvement, as the Olweus program does. However, LIFT also includes a system of rewards for groups of students who are observed practicing the good behaviors learned in LIFT sessions. This group-based reward system helps create a positive group atmosphere, supporters contend, that discourages bullying.

Another program targeted at specific grade levels is the Bullyproof curriculum developed by Lisa Sjostrum and Nan Stein of the Wellesley Centers for Women at Wellesley College, Massachusetts. Bullyproof is aimed at students in grades 4 and 5. Its 11 lessons include reading and writing exercises, role plays, and prompts for class discussions to help students explore and determine the differences between teasing and bullying (Sjostrum & Stein, 1996). Bullyproof was evaluated in a three-year research project in Austin, Texas, funded by the Centers for Disease Control, where pre- and post-tests for both teachers and students established its effectiveness.

Many other antibullying and antiharassment programs are being developed and tested in U.S. schools and even preschools, some implementing interventions with students as young as two years of age. Whether any one program will prove totally effective is doubtful, but the magnitude of the problem of bullying, harassment, and student violence, and the toll they take on students, families, and the educational community, make the search for effective strategies critically important.

Funds for implementing programs and training staff in positive behavioral interventions are often available through the federal government's Safe and Drug Free Schools program and state and local program coordinators. A report by Fight Crime: Invest in Kids cites research estimating that each high-risk juvenile prevented from adopting a life of crime saves the country between $1.7 and $2.3 million (Fox et al., 2003). Money for schools' antibullying and antiviolence programs would seem to be well spent.

Breaking the Code of Silence

Creating a school climate of safety and caring often includes breaking the code of silence. Students who are bullied are often fearful of reporting their oppressors for fear of making their situation even worse. Bystanders, too, often maintain silence because they fear they may become new or additional targets. Anonymous "tip lines" may help encourage students to report bullying, harassment, or threats that they see or hear, but students may distrust even those guarantees of anonymity. Rewards, likewise, may not be enticing enough to counter students' fears of being found out as a "tattletale" or "snitch."

A school district in Warren County, Pennsylvania, took a more direct approach. It wrote into its discipline code a miscellaneous inappropriate behavior (MIB) provision. The provision, Section IV (O) of the code, states:

> Any student who engages in inappropriate behavior, not otherwise specifically addressed in this Code, including but not limited to self-destructive behavior, behavior that may be harmful to others or the property of others, or other behavior which negatively reflects the values of this discipline code or the philosophy, goals and aims of the Warren County School District, will be subject to suspension or other disciplinary action.

The student handbook also includes a Section II, providing that "this policy may apply outside of school property . . . if there is misconduct that has a direct and immediate tendency to influence the conduct of other people while in the school room." In addition, the handbook requires that students "be willing to volunteer information in matters relating to the health, safety, and welfare of the school community and the protection of school property."

The district applied this policy when disciplining a 3rd grade student, Jedidiah Schmader, who had failed to warn school authorities that his friend intended to harm another student. Jedidiah was playing at his friend Tyler's home when he found a plastic dart with a metal tip. Tyler took the dart, telling Jedidiah that he wanted it to hurt another boy at school. Jedidiah surrendered the dart but told Tyler he did not want to hurt anybody. Jedidiah went home, but, as he later testified, he did not tell anyone because he "forgot."

The next day, Jedidiah was called to the principal's office where he was confronted with Tyler and the dart. Jedidiah admitted the dart had been his, and the principal called both boys' parents; after a conference, the principal suspended both boys for the rest of the day. Jedidiah and his parents subsequently went before a hearing officer who found the 3rd grader guilty of MIB and recommended that Jedidiah serve three days of after-school detention for 15 minutes each day. The MIB infraction was to become part of Jedidiah's permanent school record.

Jedidiah's parents appealed the hearing officer's determination in court, as provided by the Pennsylvania Education Code. The trial court ordered the school district to rescind any disciplinary action against Jedidiah and expunge the incident from his record. The school district appealed to Commonwealth Court.

In October 2002, Commonwealth Court upheld the right of the Warren County School District to discipline Jedidiah under the MIB provision of the district code. Although Jedidiah's parents argued that the code provision was unconstitutionally vague and did not put Jedidiah on notice of what behaviors it prohibited, the court took notice of "the wide range of unanticipated conduct" that could disrupt the educational process and the need for schools to have "greater flexibility" to regulate children's conduct than they would have to regulate the conduct of adults.

Judge Dante Pellegrini, in writing for the majority, forcefully stated that "any 8-year-old child knows or should know that knowledge of the intent of another child to throw a dart in order to injure a third child is 'behavior that may be harmful to others,' and, therefore, is wrong." The court saw the after-school suspension not as punishment but as a way to teach Jedidiah that he should "attempt to prevent harm from befalling another human being." Jedidiah's parents tried to appeal the Commonwealth Court's decision to the Pennsylvania Supreme Court, but their appeal was denied.

The *Schmader* decision is a strong affirmation and justification of a school district's right to compel students to work with the school community to secure the well-being of all students, especially because it followed after several earlier Pennsylvania court decisions that seemed to weaken school districts' authority to prohibit miscellaneous inappropriate behaviors. The exact language of the Warren County School District's code is extremely important. Districts that want to break the code of silence by writing legally defensible provisions into their student codes of conduct, requiring students to reveal information regarding potential harm to members of the school community or face disciplinary consequences, have an exemplar in the Warren County School District policies.

Strengthening Teacher Background Checks

Bearing in mind that students are not the only perpetrators of violence in schools, many school districts are looking to improve the screening of employees who will have close contact with students. Numerous states require only perfunctory background checks of prospective employees. For example, the *Chicago Tribune* recently reported that a typical prospective teacher background check in Illinois looks only for prior criminal convictions in Illinois and that Illinois is one of many states that do not require fingerprint checks (Rado, 2003). Several states, such as Pennsylvania and Ohio, require fingerprinting only for prospective employees coming from out-of-state. Other states, however, have adopted more stringent checks. Several require prospective teachers to reveal all arrests, even those not resulting in convictions. Vermont is moving forward with plans to post disciplinary actions against teachers on its state Department of Education Web site.

Criminal convictions, however, are only the most extreme indicators of potential problems with prospective school district employees. Many applicants for teaching, administrative, or support personnel positions in schools present glowing letters of recommendation from current or former employers. In too many cases, these letters scream, "Take this person off my hands, please." In other cases, the recommendation writer has only circumstantial evidence of an employee's poor job performance or inappropriate behavior and is afraid to put his true opinion in writing for fear of a lawsuit. He writes a letter that sidesteps any substantive information.

Simply reviewing the paper files of a prospective school employee may not be enough. Where feasible, district administrators should make a personal contact with former employers or with authors of recommendation letters. When making these personal contacts, usually by telephone, administrators on both ends of the conversation are well advised to stick to the facts and avoid opinion statements. The desire to ask for or to give an "off-the-record" assessment of the candidate's suitability for the job is strong, but any information shared in that context is not privileged and may be subpoenaed if a disgruntled applicant decides to sue after failing to be hired or being dismissed based on an "off-the-record" conversation. Telephone calls are certainly helpful, but even telephone conversations should be limited to comments based on observable or documented facts. It goes without saying that all conversations must be truthful.

Many states have laws addressing the issue of giving references for employees, particularly with respect to immunity for communications made in good faith. School districts should consider adopting and promulgating policies of their own, consonant with state laws, to give guidance to all district personnel who may be asked to provide references. Perhaps the most difficult issues in hiring or firing school employees involve candidates strongly suspected of, or actually known to be guilty of, sexual misconduct. In such cases, districts walk a thin line between potential liability for defamation and liability for negligent hiring, negligent misrepresentation, or even fraud (Hartmeister, 1997). However, aside from any threat of legal action, the havoc that just one pedophile can wreak in a district and the potential damage to students' lives mandate that districts err on the side of full factual disclosure, as the *Bennett* case discussed in Chapter 3 demonstrates.

Protecting the Accused

Whereas districts have a moral, and perhaps legal, responsibility to fully disclose suspected or known cases of sexual abuse by employees, districts also have a moral, and legal, duty to protect the reputations of teachers falsely accused by students of sexual improprieties and to resolve accusations promptly. False accusations of sexual misconduct can literally become a matter of life and death. Even nonsexual accusations of assault can so threaten a teacher's reputation that the teacher cannot cope. Ron Mayfield Jr., a teacher of English as a Second Language at the Woodrow Wilson Middle School in Roanoke, Virginia, committed suicide after he was falsely accused of assaulting one of his male students. Mayfield jumped off a bridge to his death while the investigation into the student's allegations dragged on for two weeks. District officials failed to inform him that law enforcement officials had cleared him of the charges the previous day (Dwyer, 2004).

Mayfield is not the only teacher who chose to die rather than face humiliation and professional disgrace. Innocent until proven guilty must apply in schools as well as in courts of law.

After the Trauma

Many educators and parents believe that schools are underprepared to deal with crises. A 2002 survey of school resource officers supported those opinions. Conducted by the National Association of School Resource Officers (NASRO), a professional organization representing more than 9,000 U.S. and international police officers assigned to K–12 schools, the survey indicated that most of them see significant gaps in schools' preparedness to deal with crises. Even where schools have crisis plans, they report, many of these plans are inadequate and untested. In addition, 89 percent of the 658 officers responding to the survey believed that crimes occurring on school campuses were significantly underreported.

If crises and tragedies do occur in schools, will postcrises plans be any better? How will school authorities deal effectively with victims of school violence? As with many school issues, shortages of time, money, and manpower sometimes leave schools with out-of-date policies and action plans. Psychological treatment plans have evolved over the years as more and more research has accumulated, but schools are often not privy to the most current findings.

Many victim treatment programs still advise trying to get victims to talk about what happened soon afterward, to verbalize their feelings as a result of the harm they suffered. This "critical incident stress debriefing" is designed to reduce immediate stress, prevent posttraumatic stress, and identify persons in need of further treatment. A kind of psychological triage, critical incident stress debriefing encourages victims to relate to a counselor what happened and how they felt, while the counselor reassures them that their responses were normal. Some recent studies suggest that this approach is ineffective and, in fact, may make the victim worse. Instead, clinical research now recommends distancing victims from the traumatic event or events, rather than re-exposing them to the trama by having them relate details of their experience ("After the Trauma," 2003).

Drug treatment with medicines such as beta-blockers that reduce anxiety and slow the formation of disturbing memories has been found effective and may now be recommended. New medical information like this may be slow to percolate to schools, resulting in schools' complicating the efforts of medical personnel to help victims of school-related trauma.

Experienced educators whose training in handling trauma dates to their preservice days should rely on professionals for help after episodes of school violence. Educators should not become amateur psychologists after school traumas. Trained assistance is necessary to direct and assist recovery from school-related traumas.

Final Thoughts

Bullying, harassment, and threats in schools are the outward signs that schools are not entirely happy places. Such manifestations can be traced to less apparent origins. Students who harbor the anger, bigotry, hate, contempt, poor coping skills, or inappropriate sense of entitlement that bring on those behaviors reflect the adults in society who have communicated those messages. Although the statistics on the prevalence of bullying in schools, student-on-student and teacher-on-student harassment, and school shootings and violence are daunting, cause for optimism exists.

Violent crime in the school is on the decline. Equality of access to public schools, while not totally accomplished, is the law. Equality of achievement is a national goal, embedded in the No Child Left Behind legislation. Schools are working toward being happier places.

Although problems exist, and occasionally swamp school officials' capacity to deal with them effectively, every school in the U.S. system of public education can point to positive results with significant numbers of students. Happy children outnumber the sad in nearly every school, with a few exceptions at times of extraordinary and unforeseen events. A visitor to any elementary school will see smiles, toothless grins, faces eager to learn, hands eager to help. Secondary school students may exhibit more subtle signs that they are growing in knowledge, maturing, and learning to take their places in society. Many teachers come back year after year to teach them. Is it the "nine month job"? The benefits? Experienced and dedicated teachers will tell you without hesitation, "It's the kids."

Educators have many issues to deal with on a daily basis: curriculum issues, assessment issues, pedagogical issues, social issues, and *legal* issues. Hopefully, this book has helped school personnel better understand the legal issues surrounding bullying, harassment, and student threats of violence in K–12 schools. Hopefully, the information will help them take a proactive stance toward the issues where the law allows and react in legally appropriate ways when issues require their intervention.

Schools should be happy places; they contain the hope and promises of the future.

Annotated References and Resources

Constitutional and Statutory References

• The Safe and Drug Free Schools and Communities Act of 1994, 20 U.S.C.A. § 7101, was Public Law 89-10, April 11, 1965, Title IV, as added Public Law 103-382, Title I, § 101, Oct. 20, 1994, 108 Stat. 3672. The law was amended in 2002, and is now referenced as Public Law 89-10, Title IV, Part A, as added Public Law 107-110, Title IV, § 401, January 8, 2002, 115 Stat. 1734. The Safe and Drug Free Schools and Communities Act is a federal law, but many states have passed state laws emulating the provisions at the national level.

• The Gun-Free Schools Act, 20 U.S.C.A. § 7151, is Public Law 89-10, Title IV, Part A, Subpart 3, as added Public Law 107-110, Title IV, § 401, January 8, 2002, 115 Stat. 1762.

• The No Child Left Behind Act of 2001 is Public Law 107-110, January 8, 2002, 115 Stat. 1425.

• States with antibullying laws discussed in Chapter 8 and their statutory citations are:

– Colorado, C.R.S. 22-32-109.1
– New Jersey, NJ. Stat. § 18A:37-13 through 17; 2002 N.J. ALS 83
– Pennsylvania, 18 Pa. C.S. § 2709
– Oklahoma, 70 Okl. St. § 24 –100.2 through 100.5
– Oregon, ORS § 339.250, 254, 351, 353, 356, 359, 362, 364, 700, 704; 2001 Ore. ALS 617 HB 3403
– Vermont, 16 V.S.A. § 11, 140a, 165, 166, 565, 1161a
– Virginia, Va. Code § 22.1 –279.6

• A list of all 50 states with antibullying laws "ranked" from A+ to F is available at http://www.bullypolice.org (accessed May 2004). The Bully Police rankings for the statutes discussed in the text are:

– Colorado, B
– New Jersey, A
– Pennsylvania, F
– Oklahoma, A
– Oregon, A
– Vermont, C+
– Virginia, F

Overall, antibullying statutes in eight states received ratings of A+, A, or A-; statutes in 33 states received Fs.

• States that prohibit discrimination laws based on gender orientation and their statutes:

– California, 2002 Cal ALS 506

– Connecticut, Conn. Gen. Stats. § 10-15c

– District of Columbia, D.C. Code 1981 § 1 2520

– Massachusetts, Mass. Gen. Laws Chp. 76 § 5

– Minnesota, Minn. Stat. § 363.03, subd. 5

– New Jersey, N.J. Stat. 10:5 – 12 f(1); N.J. Stat. 10:5 – 5 (l); N.J.A.B. 1874 (effective September 6, 2002; supplementing chapter 37 of Title 18 A of the New Jersey statutes)

– Vermont, 16 Vt. Stat. § 11 (a) (26); 16 Vt. Stat. § 565

– Washington, Wash. Rev. Code §§ 28 A. 320; 28 A. 600

– Wisconsin, Wis. Stat. 118.13

Court Decisions

• The three seminal student speech cases, decided by the U.S. Supreme Court in 1969–1988:

– *Tinker v. Des Moines Independent School District,* 393 U.S. 503 (1969),

– *Bethel School District No. 403 v. Fraser,* 478 U.S. 675 (1986), and

– *Hazelwood School District v. Kuhlmeier,* 484 U.S. 260 (1988).

• A.G.'s lawsuit was *S.G. ex rel. A.G. v Sayreville Board of Education,* 333 F.3d 417 (3d Cir. 2003), cert. denied, 124 S. Ct. 1040 (2004). S.G. is A.G.'s father. The petition for *certiorari* to the U.S. Supreme Court was filed June 19, 2003; the Court refused to hear the case on January 12, 2004.

• The gender orientation lawsuit that resulted in a $1.1 million settlement is *Flores v. Morgan Hill Unified School District,* 324 F.3d 1130 (9th Cir. 2003).

• The *Saxe* decision is *Saxe v. State College Area School District,* 240 F.3d 200 (3d Cir. 2001). For other examples of unconstitutionally vague and overbroad language to avoid in drafting school discipline policies, see

- *Killion v. Franklin Regional School District,* 136 F. Supp.2d 446 (W.D. Pa. 2001);
- *Sypniewski v. Warren Hills Regional Board of Education,* 307 F.3d 243 (3d Cir. 2002);
- *Coy v. Board of Education of the North Canton City Schools,* 205 F. Supp.2d 791 (N.D. Ohio 2002);
- *Flaherty v. Keystone Oaks School District,* 247 F. Supp.2d 698 (W.D. Pa. 2003); and
- *Smith v. Mount Pleasant Public School District,* 285 F. Supp.2d 987 (E.D. Mich. 2003) (discussed in Chapter 2).

• Jedidiah Schmader's case is *Schmader v. Warren County School District,* 808 A.2d 596 (Commw. Pa. 2002). His appeal to the Pennsylvania Supreme Court was denied on March 31, 2003, at 820 A.2d 163 (2002).

Journal Articles, Texts, and Commentaries

• Green, F. G. (1999). Zero tolerance strikes again. *Safer School News, 68.* The essay appears with links on the Keys to Safer Schools Web site: www.keystosaferschools.com/zero.htm (accessed May 2004).

• Christina Hyun Lough's plight was described in

- Rice, H. (2003, October 22). No slack for pencil sharpener: Katy schools sued after girl disciplined. *Houston Chronicle;* and
- Rodrigues, J. (2003, November 20). Petition targets Katy ISD on discipline. *Houston Chronicle.*

Both articles are available in the archives of the *Houston Chronicle* Web site for a fee: www.chron.com/content/archive/index.mpl (accessed May 2004).

- For documentation of other cases involving students suspended under zero tolerance policies and implications for students' due process rights, see Jenkins, J. K. & Dayton, J. (2002). Students, weapons, and due process: An analysis of zero tolerance policies in public schools. *Education Law Reporter 171*(13).

- The Advancement Project and the Civil Rights Project. (2000). *Opportunities suspended: The devastating consequences of zero tolerance and school discipline policies.* New Haven, CT: Authors. Available at www.civilrightsproject.harvard.edu/research/discipline/opport_suspended.php (accessed May 2004).

- Spital, S. (2003). Restoring Brown's promise of equality after *Alexander v. Sandoval:* Why we can't wait. Harvard Blackletter Law Journal 19(93).

- Marksamer, J. and Joslin, C. (2004). *Harassment and discrimination: A legal overview.* [Online] Available at www.nclrights.org/publications/ha-legaloverview.htm (accessed May 2004).

- Human Rights Campaign Foundation. (2004). Transgender basics [Online]. Available at www.hrc.org/Template.cfm?Section=Transgender_Basics (accessed May 2004).

- Pogash, C. (2004, January 7). California school district settles harassment suit by gay students. *New York Times.* Available with registration at www.nytimes.com/2004/01/07/education/07SETT.html (accessed May 2004).

- Robelon, E.W. (2003, September 24). States report few schools as dangerous. *Education Week 23*(4), p. 1.

- New Jersey's antibullying law was described in Bitman, T. (2003, November 11). N.J. gets tougher on bullying in schools. *The Philadelphia Inquirer.* p. B10.

- Olweus, D., Limber, S., & Mihelic, S. F. (1999). *Blueprints for violence prevention, book nine: Bullying prevention program.* Boulder, CO: Center for the Study and Prevention of Violence. Excerpts available at www.colorado.edu/cspv/blueprints/model/programs/BPP.html (accessed May 2004).

- The LIFT program is described in Fox, J. A., Elliot, D. S., Kerlikowske, R. G., Newman, S. A., & Christeson, W. (2003). *Bullying prevention is crime prevention.* Washington, DC: Fight Crime: Invest in Kids. Available as a PDF file at www.fightcrime.org/reports/BullyingReport.pdf (accessed May 2004).
- Sjostrum, L. & Stein, N. D. (1996). *Bullyproof: A teacher's guide on teasing and bullying for use with 4th and 5th grade students.* Wellesley, MA: Center for Research on Women.
- Criticisms of teacher background checks were documented in Rado, D. (2003, November 30). Teachers can hide criminal records. *The Chicago Tribune.* Available for a fee at www. chicagotribune.com (accessed May 2004).
- Hartmeister, F. (1997). Handling requests for employment references: Evaluating awareness among the pitfalls and pendulums. *Education Law Reporter 119*(1).
- Dwyer, T. (2004, February 12). A false accusation, and a fateful decision. *Washington Post.* p. B01. Available for a fee at www. washingtonpost.com (accessed May 2004).
- The NASRO survey is reported at www.schoolsecurity.org/resources/nasro_survey_2002.html (accessed May 2004).
- After the trauma: What doesn't help and what may. (2003, November). *Harvard Mental Health Letter, 20*(5). p. 5. Available for a fee at www.health.harvard.edu (accessed May 2004).

Internet Resources

Resources for Preventing Bullying

American Academy of Child and Adolescent Psychiatry
www.aacap.org/publications/factsfam/80.htm

American Academy of Pediatrics
www.aap.org/advocacy/archives/aug01school.htm

American Psychological Association Help Center
www.helping.apa.org/warningsigns/recognizing.html

Child and Adolescent Violence Research at the National Institute of
   Mental Health
www.nimh.nih.gov/publicat/violenceresfact.cfm

Child Abuse Preventive Services—The Child Safety Institute
www.kidsafe-caps.org/bullies.html

Committee for Children: Information on Bullying and Sexual
   Harassment
www.cfchildren.org/bully.html

International Education and Resource Network
www.bullying.org

National Association of School Psychologists
www.nasponline.org/factsheets/bullying-fs.html

National Education Association: National Bullying Awareness Campaign
http://nea.org/issues/safescho/bullying

National School Safety Center
www.nssc1.org

National Resource Center for Safe Schools
www.safetyzone.org

U.S. Department of Education
www.ed.gov/pubs202/crime2001/6.asp?nav=1

U.S. Department of the Secret Service
www.secretservice.gov/ntac.htm

Resources for Dealing with Harassment in the School Setting

Sexual Harassment Resources

Feminist Majority Foundation
www.feminist.org/911/harass.html

Men's Issues Pages
www.menweb.org/throop/harass/harass.html

National Institute of Justice: Primer on Sexual Harassment
www.ncjrs.org/txtfiles/harass.txt

Sexual Harassment in Schools Project at Wellesley Centers for Women
www.wcwonline.org/harassment/resources.html

Sexual Harassment Resources
http://library.uncg.edu/depts/docs/us/harass.html

Women's Studies Database: Gender Issues
www.mith2.umd.edu/WomensStudies/GenderIssues/
    SexualHarassment

U.S. Department of Education: Office for Civil Rights
www.ed.gov/about/offices/list/ocr/sexharassresources.html

U.S. Equal Employment Opportunity Commission
www.eeoc.gov/facts/fs-sex.html

Other Forms of Harassment

Anti-Discrimination Board: Race Discrimination: Your Rights
www.lawlink.nsw.gov.au/adb.nsf/pages/race

U.S. Department of Labor
www.dol.gov/dol/topic/discrimination/agedisc.htm

U.S. Equal Employment Commission: Facts About Age Discrimination
www.eeoc.gov/facts/age.html

U.S. Equal Employment Commission: Facts About Race/Color
    Discrimination
www.eeoc.gov/facts/fs-race.html

Resources Dealing with Student Violence

American Psychological Association
http://helping.apa.org/warningsigns

ASCD: Health in Education Initiative
www.ascd.org/cms/index.cfm?TheViewID=2173

California Department of Education: Safe Schools and Violence
    Prevention
www.cde.ca.gov/spbranch/safety

Center for Effective Collaboration and Practice
http://cecp.air.org/guide/Default.htm
www.air.org/cecp/school_violence.htm

Center for the Prevention of School Violence
www.ncdjjdp.org/cpsv/cpsv.htm

Center for the Study and Prevention of Violence
www.colorado.edu/cspv

ERIC Digests: Improving School Violence Prevention Programs through Meaningful Evaluation. ERIC/CUE Digest Number 132.
www.ericfacility.net/databases/ERIC_Digests/ed417244.html

Family Concerns: School Safety
www.parentingresources.ncjrs.org/familyconcerns/schoolsafety.html

Family Education Network: School Violence Prevention Plan
www.teachervision.fen.com/lesson-plans/lesson-3006.html

National Education Center: School Safety
www.nea.org/schoolsafety/resources-schoolsafety.html

National Mental and Education Health Center
www.naspcenter.org/safe_schools/safeschools.htm

National School Safety Center
www.nssc1.org

National Youth Violence Prevention Resource Center (NYVPRC)
www.safeyouth.org/scripts/index.asp

Office of Juvenile Justice and Delinquency Prevention
http://ojjdp.ncjrs.org/resources/school.html
www.ojjdp.ncjrs.org/pubs/fact.html#fs200127

Ribbon of Promise National Campaign to End School Violence
www.ribbonofpromise.org/research.html

Safe and Drug Free Schools: School Violence & Prevention
Implementing Prevention Programs and Policies
www.ncela.gwu.edu/pathways/safeschools/programs.htm

School-Based Violence Prevention Programs
www.ucalgary.ca/resolve/violenceprevention/English

Selected Bibliography of School Violence Resources
www.lib.umich.edu/socwork/schoolviolence.html

UCLA School Mental Health Project
http://smhp.psych.ucla.edu

U.S. Department of Health and Human Services: School Violence
    Prevention
www.mentalhealth.org/schoolviolence/links.asp

U.S. Department of Justice
www.usdoj.gov/youthviolence.htm

Resources for Dealing with Student Suicides

The Surgeon General's Call to Action, a blueprint for addressing suicide
    by Awareness, Intervention and Methodology (AIM), and other CDC
    publications
www.cdc.gov/ncipc/factsheets/suifacts.htm, and www.sg.gov/library/
    calltoaction

National Strategy for Suicide Prevention: Goals and Objectives for
    Action
www.mentalhealth.org/suicideprevention

Reporting on Suicide: Recommendations for the Media
www.afsp.org/education/newsrecommendations.htm

American Association of Suicidology
www.suicidology.org

American Foundation for Suicide Prevention
www.afsp.org

National Institute of Mental Health (NIMH)
www.nimh.nih.gov

National Youth Violence Prevention Resource Center
www.safeyouth.org

Suicide Prevention Advocacy Network (SPAN)
www.spanusa.org

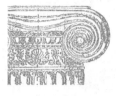

Index

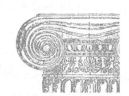

About the Author

KATHLEEN CONN IS AN EDUCATOR AND public school administrator as well as a lawyer and member of the Pennsylvania Bar. Conn earned her Ph.D. in Physics/ Biology at Bryn Mawr College, studying molecular dynamics with pulsed nuclear magnetic resonance techniques. She completed postdoctoral work in the cell biology of cancer metastasis at Lankenau Medical Research Center in Philadelphia. She has taught science and problem solving at the secondary, college, and graduate levels, both in the United States and abroad. Conn also has been a delegate to international conferences on physics education and a member of the Advisory Council for both the Mechanical Universe High School Adaptation (MUHSA) and the Comprehensive Conceptual Curriculum for Physics (C3P), two NSF-sponsored exemplary precollege physics curriculum projects.

Conn returned to student status to earn her J.D. degree at Widener University School of Law, Evening Division, while making the transition to public school administration. For the past eight years, she has been a K–12 curriculum supervisor in the West Chester Area School District.

Conn is the author of *The Internet and the Law: What Educators Need to Know* (ASCD, 2002) and numerous journal articles in the areas of science research, science education, and education law. She is a frequent presenter at local and national conferences of the National Science Teachers' Association, Technology Education Association, and the Education Law Association, and consults on issues of safety in the science classroom, teacher liability, and Internet issues in public schools. She has also presented papers at science and education conferences in Canada and Europe.

Related ASCD Resources

Bullying and Harassment: A Legal Guide for Educators

At the time of publication, the following ASCD resources were available; for the most up-to-date information about ASCD resources, go to www.ascd.org. ASCD stock numbers are noted in parentheses.

Audio

Beyond Bullying by Beth Madison (#203153 audiotape; #503246 CD)

The Bully, The Bullied, The Bystander: Breaking the Cycle of Violence by Barbara Coloroso (#202145 audiotape)

The Internet and the Law in Public Schools by Kathleen Conn (#203135 audiotape; #503228 CD)

Networks

Visit the ASCD Web site (www.ascd.org) and search for "networks" for information about professional educators who have formed groups around topics like "Gay, Lesbian, Bisexual, Transgendered and Allied Issues In Education Network" and "Hispanic/Latino American Critical Issues." Look in the "Network Directory" for current facilitators' addresses and phone numbers.

Online Resources

Visit ASCD's Web site (www.ascd.org) for the following professional development opportunities:

Education Topic: *School Safety* (free)

Professional Development Online: *Conflict Resolution and Embracing Diversity, Respecting Others*, among others (for a small fee; password protected)

Print Products

The School Law Handbook: What Every Leader Needs to Know by William C. Bosher, Jr., Kate R. Kaminski, and Richard S. Vacca (#102114)

The First Amendment in Schools by Charles C. Haynes, Sam Chaltain, John E. Ferguson, Jr., David L. Hudson, Jr., and Oliver Thomas (#103054)

The Internet and the Law: What Educators Need to Know by Kathleen Conn (#102119)

Educational Leadership: Understanding the Law (entire issue, December 2001/January 2002) Excerpted articles online free; entire issue online and accessible to ASCD members

The Respectful School: How Students and Teachers Can Conquer Hate and Harassment by Stephen L. Wessler with William Preble (#103006)

Video

Teacher as Community Builder (Tape 3 of *The Teacher Series*) (#401084)

For more information, visit us on the World Wide Web (http://www.ascd.org), send an e-mail message to member@ascd.org, call the ASCD Service Center (1-800-933-ASCD or 703-578-9600, then press 2), send a fax to 703-575-5400, or write to Information Services, ASCD, 1703 N. Beauregard St., Alexandria, VA 22311-1714 USA.